FOOD FOR HEROES

Compiled by Squadron Leader Jon Pullen

and the Food for Heroes Team

Published by Accent Press Ltd – 2009

Recipes and heroes © Individual contributors – 2009

Compilation © Jon Pullen – 2009

ISBN 9781906373801

Every effort has been made to ensure that the recipes in this book are the contributors' own work and to obtain the appropriate permissions for photographs used. Please accept our apologies for any errors and omissions, which we will be very happy to correct when Food for Heroes is reprinted.

Every recipe starts with a creative talent and our thanks go to all those chefs, both professional and amateur, who have influenced our recipes.

Printed and bound in the UK by Butler Tanner and Dennis, Frome and London

Paper supply supported by Burgo Group and Denmaur Independent Papers Ltd.

Contents

Foreword by Kate Adie v

Introduction vii

Starters and Soups 1

Snacks and Salads 13

Vegetarian 37

Seafood 51

Poultry 79

Pork 107

Lamb 117

Beef 143

Game and Sausages 177

Puddings and Baking 189

Acknowledgements 235

Index 237

To absent friends

Foreword by Kate Adie

Sausage. Tomato. Eggs. Fried bread. A mountain of baked beans. I went off to war and invaded Iraq on a very full stomach.

I had never given much thought to the relationship of food to fighting, in spite of Napoleon's army marching on its stomach. Not until I found myself in Saudi Arabia with forty-three thousand British troops waiting to liberate Kuwait. Only then did I begin to realize that the field kitchen loomed large in our daily thoughts. We needed energy, we needed a break from the trench-digging and convoy-driving, and we needed a few minutes of chatting and griping and jokes and news of home. The mysteries of field rations came later: Cheese(Tinned) and Biscuits(Brown) and the preponderance of Pilchards in Tomato Sauce were nevertheless welcome when you sheltered under an armoured vehicle and scraped the sharp and grubby sand off the cans and your hands and face. And the provisioning owes a lot to one of my heroes – Florence Nightingale, whose determination to stop the British Army in the Crimea being killed by its own incompetent superiors led to a revolution in military administration.

Nightingale, forever associated with lamp-lit walks through the crowded wards in Scutari, started her mission by spending a great deal of her time staring into cooking pots. The British soldiers she first encountered were not dying of wounds so much as of starvation, dirt and neglect. The rationing system was perverse, the cooking consisted of cursory boiling, and the food itself was frequently inedible. Unlike most of the military senior staff, she connected the mortality rate to the disgusting conditions and revolting diet. It seems the most obvious of observations, but she battled for years to have conditions improved and met ceaseless opposition from the government and its officials, and also from the general public. One of the reasons was that the public did not think much of the British soldier: drunken, brutish, Wellington's 'mere scum of the earth'. Nightingale's work in the Crimea transformed this image because she transformed the soldiery, teaching officers to respect their men and giving the men better conditions.

However, even when servicemen and women today are held in much higher regard as professionals, there is still that tendency to take them for granted, or provide only the bare minimum of support – even forget them – as they put their lives on the line in circumstances which are hard for the rest of us at home to imagine. That is why we still need to insist that they receive the best possible treatment and care. Florence Nightingale, I am sure, would be urging today that we should all 'do our bit' at home, making sure that those who risk their lives in the Services are not be neglected. She fought her battles on a stomach of plain food and often limited rations, so I would hesitate to offer her a recipe.

However, in 1856 she wrote that she was sustained by 'a little brandy and water' as she endured freezing weather and deprivation at Balaclava. Let us raise a glass to her, our troops and the other Heroes in this book.

Introduction

I guess it all started with a meeting in November 2007 about 19 months before this book's publication. I had just completed a four-month tour in Iraq as part of the Helicopter Force based out of Basra and, like so many of us, I had been extremely moved by what a new charity, "Help for Heroes", was trying to do. I wanted to help.

My experience in Iraq must have been much the same as all the others who were part of Operation Telic in the Summer of 2007: 50C temperature; a rocket or two (there had been over 400 fired into Basra Airport during my four-month tour); a massive interest from the UK media as we began reducing operations in the city and of course a LOT of time in the gym. Where my experience was a bit different from others' was the job we were doing. Part of our role was to recover injured servicemen and women from the field and get them to the medical facility as quickly as possible. This is often referred to as the Golden Hour wherein an injured person's chances of survival are greatly improved if he or she can reach a medical facility within 60 minutes. As an RAF Engineer who in the past had operated a long way from the front, I had never been so close to so many injured men and women; this was where the book was born.

Anyway, back to that meeting. I had invited seven people I thought might be interested: Sergeant Al Bowman, a communications engineer who had already raised over £2000 running charity auctions; Sergeant Dawn Bailey, one of RAF Aldergrove's chefs and a really positive individual; Captain Chris Underhill, who worked in the station printing facility, and knew how to get things on to paper; Flight Lieutenant Paul Duke, an officer

I knew well who ran the station photography section; Ms Gillian George, a civil servant and a superb administrator; Flight Lieutenant Tom Humphreys who ran our station IT system and Flight Lieutenant John Gorman, an officer with a reputation for getting things done. I explained the concept of what we were going to do:

we were going to raise £100,000.

we were going to rock the literary world with a cookery book.

there were going to be celebrities involved.

"OK who knows anything about writing a book?" Complete silence but, critically, nobody laughed or left the room. I think, looking back, the biggest indication of our detachment from the reality of our ambition and complete ignorance of how books are created was the fact that we were going to have the whole project finished in four months … how we laugh now!

From that point the concept grew, our team expanded, and, crucially, we were given £200 by RAF Aldergrove's Charity Committee to help with our costs. Twenty letters a week were sent out to agents, managers, publishing agents, personal secretaries, public relations managers, and other celebrity-protecting sentinels I never even knew existed (I have learned that phrases like "he'll call you back," "he's with a client at the moment," and the dreaded "he's away from his desk right now," are all euphemisms for "sorry not interested"). After four weeks without a single response, positive or negative, a heavy blanket of doubt was beginning to settle on the team. Then we received an email from Ewan McGregor, who has connections to the armed forces and had recently returned from Basra. One down and only 99 more contributions required, but we celebrated nonetheless. Other highlights were Ainsley Harriot singing to me down the phone, a surreal conversation with Tony Blair's office about why our previous PM refused to serve Chocolate Roulade to Mahatma Gandhi and my personal favourite telephone call, "Hello, I'm Mrs Wilkinson, I'm Jonny's Mother."

So that's where it started. The project has been challenging (we all have day jobs and very supportive bosses), however, the overriding sense has been one of the privilege of having had the opportunity to meet some truly incredible people. In the pages that follow you will find some familiar names and some not so familiar. Every serviceman and woman in the book has earned the right to be included as a hero, having served in at least one combat zone; every major British conflict from the first world war to Afghanistan is represented. Contributors were asked who their heroes are (living or dead, fictional or real), why they are their heroes and, given the opportunity, what they would feed them. The result is an extraordinary mixture that blends our fascination with food and heroism in a way that is in places amusing and moving but always captivating. It has been an incredible journey that has given us all a chance to challenge our preconceptions of

what heroism means to us and of course given us an opportunity to help Bryn and Emma Parry and the rest of the Help for Heroes team with the quite extraordinary work they are doing by donating all profits and royalties from this book to Help for Heroes.

So thank you for purchasing Food for Heroes and in so doing helping our national heroes who have been injured serving their country. While you are flicking through the book or trying the recipes please give a small thought to what these individuals have done for us and of course you might like to consider for yourself:

What would you feed your hero?

Squadron Leader Jon Pullen

starters & soups

Dame Eileen Atkins
Writer and Actress

My Hero
Gandhi

The political and spiritual leader of India and the Indian independence movement, Gandhi was an advocate of resistance to tyranny through mass civil disobedience, founded upon total non-violence. This led India to independence and inspired movements for civil rights and freedom across the world. He is officially honoured in India as the Father of the Nation on his birthday, the 2nd October. Gandhi was a practitioner of non-violence and advocated that others do the same. He lived modestly in a self-sufficient residential community and wore the traditional Indian dhoti and shawl, woven with yarn he had hand spun. He ate simple vegetarian food, and also undertook long fasts as means of both self-purification and social protest.

After campaigning in South Africa for the rights of Indian ex-patriots, he assumed leadership of the Indian National Congress. He led nationwide campaigns for easing poverty, expanding women's rights, building religious and ethnic harmony, ending untouchability, increasing economic self-reliance, but above all for achieving independence for India. Gandhi famously led Indians in protesting the British-imposed salt tax with the 400 kilometre (249 mile) Dandi Salt March in 1930.

He was imprisoned for many years, on numerous occasions, in both South Africa and India. His bravery to risk persecution by campaigning in solely non-violent means shows utter dedication and belief.

His ability to make so many follow in his footsteps, forging the modern India, singles him out as a truly remarkable man.

Baked Figs with Walnuts and Blue Cheese

DIFFICULTY LEVEL	PREPARATION TIME	COOKING TIME	SERVES
MODERATE	20 MINUTES	4-6 MINUTES	4

Ingredients

4 fresh figs
handful of walnuts
75g dolcelatta cheese
80ml double cream
8 slices parma ham (prosciutto or bacon can be used as an alternative)
2 tbsp balsamic vinegar
1 tbsp lemon juice
olive oil
black pepper
lettuce of your choice

Method

1 Pre-heat the oven to 200C/400F/Gas Mark 6.

2 Cut a deep cross into the figs and pinch together to open.

3 Cut a small slice from the bottom so they stand upright.

4 Place on an oiled baking sheet.

5 Finely chop the walnuts.

6 In a bowl mix together the dolcelatta, a little double cream and most of the walnuts.

7 Season the mixture and stuff the figs generously with the mixture.

8 Wrap the figs tightly with a slice or two of the parma ham.

9 Bake in the oven for 4–6 minutes, or until the cheese mixture is beginning to melt.

10 Meanwhile take the balsamic vinegar, a squeeze of lemon and the remaining walnuts and whisk with olive oil and black pepper.

11 Dress with lettuce and finish with the balsamic dressing.

My Hero

Major Mordechai Anielewicz

Commander of the Jewish Fighting Organisation (ZOB)

On 19 April 1943 the ZOB launched the Warsaw Ghetto Uprising: the first military action in German-occupied Europe.

About two thousand Jewish fighters armed with only pistols, hand grenades, Molotov cocktails and a handful of automatic rifles faced the German military might with its artillery units, armoured vehicles, chemical weapons and flame throwers.

Anielewicz organised, armed and inspired his fighters. He knew their fight was doomed to military failure; but history has judged the uprising to have been a heroic action for the Warsaw Ghetto Jews, who battled not only against Hitler's Germany, but also for their honour and human dignity.

Chicken Noodle Soup

Ingredients

half a boiling fowl
1 uncooked chicken carcass
200g chopped chicken giblets
 and turkey necks
6 litres water
5 carrots
5 celery sticks
2 parsnips
1 swede
2 onions
2 tomatoes
3 chicken stock cubes
2 tsp salt
3 bay leaves
8 black pepper corns
150g egg noodles

DIFFICULTY LEVEL	PREPARATION TIME	COOKING TIME	SERVES
EASY	20 MINUTES	3 HOURS	8-10

Method

1 Cut the chicken into biggish pieces.

2 Peel and thinly slice all the vegetables, except the onions, and just halve the tomato.

3 Put all the ingredients into a large pot, keeping the onions unpeeled and leaving out the noodles for now.

4 Bring to the boil and simmer for three hours, skimming the scum off the top from time to time.

5 Remove from the heat and cool a little.

6 Strain the contents of the pot, return the vegetables to the strained soup and save the chicken meat for future use. Throw away all the other ingredients.

7 Let the soup cool down for at least 12 hours in a refrigerator to infuse all the flavours.

8 When you are ready to use it, reheat the soup. Break up the noodles a little and add to the hot soup, simmer for a few minutes to soften the noodles and serve very hot.

There are as many recipes for chicken noodle soup as there are Jewish grandmothers and mamas. From what I remember this is my grandmother's version.

WARRANT OFFICER
ANDREW WISEMAN

Andre Weizmann was born a Polish Jew in Berlin in 1923. Watching the changing climate of 1930s Germany, his father took Andrew and his American wife to Warsaw for a safer life. By August 1939 war was on the horizon and Andrew was sent to England for his safety; unfortunately his father, unable to get an exit visa, could not join him and subsequently lost his life in a concentration camp.

Aged 16, Andrew arrived in England and, although he was fluent in Polish, German and Russian, he could hardly speak any English so he spent the next two years at a school in Hampshire learning the language. In 1941 Andrew volunteered to join the Royal Air Force as aircrew and trained as a Sergeant Observer in South Africa before eventually flying in Halifax bombers out of Leconfield in Yorkshire. 'I was neither military-minded nor had I any great desire to defend the Empire; for me the war was personal, an opportunity to fight for my family,' he says.

In April 1944, when he had had less than a hundred flying hours, his squadron was tasked on an operation targeting railway yards, stations and bridges in order to deny the Germans the capability of transporting reinforcements to the coast in readiness for the Allied invasion of mainland Europe. During the sortie, his Halifax was attacked on its unguarded underbelly by a Messerschmitt 210, causing the aircraft to catch fire and career out of control. WO Wiseman bailed out with three other members of the crew, unfortunately three of their comrades were

not so lucky and are today buried in a small cemetery in Poix-de-Picardie. He evaded capture for two days and on the third night approached a French farmer, asking for help. The farmer, facing the death penalty if he was caught aiding a British airman, led Andrew to a nearby village and pointed to a small house telling him that the occupants would assist him. After he knocked at the door a German soldier appeared; with his perfect German, Andrew attempted to bluff his way out of the situation, unfortunately his RAF uniform gave him away and he was arrested. Three weeks later, after interrogation, Andrew Wiseman entered the North Camp of Stalag Luft 3 under guard, one month after the Great Escape.

What he encountered was a camp in shock, having just learned that 50 of the officers who had escaped through the tunnel whose entrance was in Hut 104 had been murdered by the Gestapo. Hut 104 was no different from the other huts on the camp but happened to be chosen for tunnel 'Harry' due to its proximity to the wire. On 24th March 1944 seventy-six personnel had entered the tunnel making their bid for freedom.

WO Wiseman left Stalag Luft 3 in January 1945 as part of what later became known as the 'long march' in which thousands of Allied prisoners were force-marched westwards towards Spremberg, east of Berlin. The appalling weather, aggravated by the fact that the PoWs were ill-prepared for the minus 20 degree temperatures, meant that hundreds died from exhaustion, malnutrition and

disease. Andrew was eventually liberated by the Russians in April 1945.

Andrew finished his career as an Intelligence Officer serving in Berlin, the city of his birth, and was demobbed in 1947. On return to England, his exceptional language skills helped him secure a position in the BBC before eventually becoming the producer of the science TV show, Tomorrow's World.

Since then, Hut 104 has become a symbol of RAF resistance, determination, courage and bloody-mindedness. Sixty years later some of the old inmates of Stalag Luft 3 and a team of servicemen, led by Air Commodore Charles Clarke, decided to rebuild Hut 104.

They raised over £70,000 from contributions from the public, RAF stations and ex POWs and it was opened on the site of Stalag Luft 3 in Zagen, Poland in October 2008. In March 2009 Andrew joined 12 other ex-PoWs to commemorate the 65th anniversary of the Great Escape, accompanied by 40 of today's Royal Air Force personnel.

Like many ordinary men and women who have lived through extraordinary times, Andrew is reticent about speaking of his wartime experiences. When asked by his grandchildren what he did in the war, with typical understatement he replies: 'I survived and I was lucky.'

When asked by his grandchildren what he did in the war, with typical understatement he replies: 'I survived and I was lucky.'

7

My Hero
Cassius Clay

One of my early heroes was Cassius Clay, even before he became Muhammad Ali. It was in the late 1960s; I remember staying up all night to watch the so called "Rumble in the Jungle" when Ali fought George Foreman and beat the champion. It was so exciting, as it was probably one of the earliest live broadcasts of a boxing match and because of the time difference we could watch it after service! He has always been an inspiration to me, because of his sheer determination to win; his achievements were absolutely incredible and he proved that whoever you are, anything is possible if you want it badly enough. Even today, although he is so ill, he has such dignity and a great presence.

I met him, many years ago, he was one of those people that did not disappoint. It was a really exciting moment to meet such an outstanding sportsman. He literally came off the plane and came directly to the kitchen and we had lunch together; the dish that I have chosen is in fact exactly what I cooked for Mohammed Ali all those years ago.

Hot and Sour Soup with Fish

Ingredients

3 stalks lemon grass
1 thumb-size piece ginger
1 small onion
50g oyster or button mushrooms
1 medium tomato
2 limes
125–150g white fish
1 litre white chicken or fish stock
1 tsp Thai roasted chilli paste (optional)
3 fresh or frozen kaffir lime leaves
3–5 bird's eye chillies
½–1 tbsp Thai fish sauce
small handful fresh coriander leaves (optional)

Remind your guests that the lemongrass, whole chillies, ginger and lime leaves should not be eaten!

Hot and Sour Soup with Fish

DIFFICULTY LEVEL	PREPARATION TIME	COOKING TIME	SERVES
EASY	30 MINUTES	15 MINUTES	4

Method

1 Remove tough outer skin of lemon grass, lightly smash and cut into 3cm lengths.

2 Peel and slice the ginger and lightly smash.

3 Peel and coarsely chop the onion.

4 Thickly slice the mushrooms and cut the tomato into large chunks.

5 Take 3 tablespoons of juice from the limes.

6 Cut the fish in half, if you want to make more pieces.

7 Put the stock on the heat and stir in the Thai paste until dissolved.

8 Add the lemongrass, ginger and onion.

9 When the stock comes to the boil, lower the heat slightly and simmer for a few minutes.

10 Add the fish, mushrooms and tomato to the stock and simmer gently for 2–3 minutes.

11 Add the lime leaves and continue simmering for 2–3 minutes or until the fish has turned opaque, then remove from the heat.

12 Add the whole chillies, lime juice and fish sauce and stir to mix. Taste and adjust the seasoning.

13 If you want more chilli heat, break one/two of the chillies into pieces, before adding to the soup.

14 Leave to stand for several minutes, and then add coriander leaves, if using. Serve the soup hot.

Captain Eamonn Sullivan
Intensive Care Nursing Captain, Queen Alexandra's Royal Army Nursing Corps (Territorial Army)

My Hero

My Grand-uncle: Private William Moroney

2 Battalion Royal Irish Regiment (RIR)

I suspect that Uncle Willie would have liked this soup. We both come from the same part of Ireland, Waterford in the South East, famous for, amongst other things, its deep harbour and world-class fishing.

I never met Uncle Willie; in fact he 'disappeared' from our family in 1914 and wasn't found again until 2004 when by chance my father came across some family papers detailing his existence. With the exception of his broken-hearted mother, Willie had been erased from our family's memory and history. He had simply 'gone away' in 1914 and had never come back.

Willie had joined his local Waterford Regiment – the Royal Irish Regiment (RIR) – and was sent to France. He survived the Battle of the Marne and the 2nd Battalion's virtual annihilation at the Battle of Le Philly in October 1914.

On 24 of May 1915 Willie was critically wounded in a German gas attack at Bellewarde Ridge. There were 380 RIR men listed as killed or wounded in that gas attack. One of the immediate RIR fatalities was Private John Condon, a Waterford boy listed by the Commonwealth War Graves Commission as the 'youngest known (British) battle casualty of the war': John Condon died at the age of fourteen.

Willie survived the initial attack but died four days later of his gas wounds at a nearby Field Hospital. I think of Willie and the other men now and again, and I also think of the hundreds of gas casualties overwhelming the Field Hospital and the nurses and doctors doing their best to alleviate the suffering in the most primitive and horrific conditions imaginable.

Uncle Willie is my hero. He was fighting a war on two fronts – one in Ireland against the complex political situation at that time, and one against the Germans – fighting both against all odds and for what he strongly believed was the right thing to do.

Coastal Comfort Soup

Ingredients

½ onion
2 shallots
400g potatoes
25g butter
600ml milk
300ml water
150ml double cream
small glass white wine
450g undyed smoked haddock
300g flaked hot smoked salmon
sea salt
white pepper
parsley oil
1 langoustine

DIFFICULTY LEVEL	PREPARATION TIME	COOKING TIME	SERVES
MODERATE	20 MINUTES	25 MINUTES	4

Method

1 Finely chop the onion and shallots. Melt the butter, adding the onions and shallots. Saute for a few minutes and place to the side.

2 Wash, peel and cut the potatoes into small cubes. Mix the milk and water and bring to the boil.

3 Add the potatoes, then reduce the heat and simmer for 10 minutes.

4 Place the haddock fillets on top of the mixture and cover with the small glass of wine to poach, until the skin peels away and the haddock can be easily flaked, then remove the haddock and set to the side.

5 Now gently mix and mash the soup to the desired density, you can blend it down for a softer lighter soup.

6 Add seasoning and cream to attain the desired taste, then add the flaked haddock.

7 To serve, add a tablespoon of flaked hot smoked salmon in the middle and a grilled langoustine to sit proudly on top, surrounded by a drizzle of parsley oil.

snacks & salads

Mucked-Up Cheese • Egg and Chip Banjo • Full Tradition

...p • Egg Mayonnaise Sandwiches and Homemade Cris...

...Man's Chilli Tortillas • Spicy Chicken with Almonds and A...

...ockets • Greek-Style Burgers • "Nutter" not a Chicken • H...

...alad • Pan Fried Halloumi • Mucked-Up Cheese • Egg a...

...Full Traditional English Fry-Up • Egg Mayonnaise Sand...

...Homemade Crisps • Hungry Man's Chilli Tortillas • Spicy

...Almonds and Apricots Pitta Pockets • Greek-Style Burge...

...not a Chicken • Herby Coucous Salad • Pan Fried Hallou...

...Greek-Style Burgers • "Nutter" not a Chicken • Herby C...

My Hero
Lord Mountbatten

At the time I was in the Far East I would say that Lord Mountbatten was a hero of mine. He was serving as the Allied Commander, South East Asia Command (SEAC), a position he held until 1946. He and General William Slim seemed to be the only ones at the time who were interested in the 'Forgotten 14th Army'.

The 'Forgotten 14th Army' was named due to the relatively little press it received at home, despite being the single largest Army in the world at that time.

LAC Lancaster was a Motor Boat Crewman, shipped out of England in 1943 via Duran and Bombay to Colombo, Ceylon. After 18 'boring' months, he volunteered to join the RAF in Manilla as part of 230 Squadron. He sailed to Akyab in Burma where flying actually took place, and then on to the Pegu River near Rangoon for more flying.

After a period he was posted to Penang where he completed three years. He was then shipped back to England and finally 'demobbed' in 1947.

Admiral Lord Louis Mountbatten sitting at his desk (TR 1230) by permission of the Imperial War Museum

Mucked-Up Cheese

Ingredients

200g mature cheddar cheese
200g fresh breadcrumbs
200ml milk
1 tsp English mustard
2 slices thick white bread
lemon wedges and chopped fresh
parsley to garnish

Method

1 Grate the cheese and mix all ingredients (except the bread) in a saucepan. Put over a low heat and gently bring to the boil, stirring all the time.

2 When the mixture heats up it becomes thick and pasty in consistency. Toast the bread on one side, turn over and spread the mixture on the other, using up all the mixture.

3 Put it back under the grill and grill until golden brown, eat immediately and enjoy!

DIFFICULTY LEVEL	PREPARATION TIME	COOKING TIME	SERVES
VERY EASY	5 MINUTES	5 MINUTES	1

Bryn Parry
Co-Founder and Chief Executive of Help for Heroes

My Hero
Lance Bombardier Ben Parkinson

Put on your body armour, pull up a sandbag and get that lantern swinging, this is one for all the old dinosaurs like me.

South Armagh, 1981: The helicopter brings you back to Bessbrook after a five-day operation in 'bandit country'; you are cold, wet and very hungry. You unload; dump your 'bergen' and squelch down to the cookhouse. You stir five sugars into a mug of hot tea and make an egg banjo.... Suddenly the world starts to look a whole lot better.

My hero is Lance Bombardier Ben Parkinson 7 (Parachute) Regiment Royal Horse Artillery. Ben has survived thirty-seven separate injuries including the loss of both legs as well as brain damage, and yet he is determined to stay in the Army.

He was the original inspiration behind the formation of Help for Heroes.

Egg and Chip Banjo

Ingredients

**2 pieces soft white bread
(or a nice soft bap)
big scoop of chips
2 eggs
red or brown sauce**

Method

1 Butter the bread/roll.

2 Cook the chips in a hot fryer until crispy about 5–10 minutes.

3 Shallow fry the eggs.

4 Place one egg onto the bread, top with chips and add another egg.

5 Then add the sauce of your choice.

6 Top with bread.

7 See if you can eat it without getting egg running down your fingers!!!!

DIFFICULTY LEVEL	PREPARATION TIME	COOKING TIME	SERVES
EASY	1 MINUTES	5–10 MINUTES	1

The Egg Banjo has been a staple diet of all 3 services for years, traditionally served at the end of operations and exercises. It is so named due to the method used when eating it: take hold of the Banjo in both hands and take a huge bite. The eggs will burst and squirt out in all directions; while lifting the Banjo to the side with one hand, you will make a frantic brushing motion with your spare hand to wipe the mess off the front of your shirt ... looking just like George Formby playing the banjo.

My Hero
Roberto Duran

Roberto Duran was a natural-born fighter who grew up in the tough streets of Panama. The Latin legend learned to fight at a young age and turned pro at sixteen. He went on to become perhaps the best and most inspirational fighter of all time. He declared to the press, 'I was born to be champion of the world,' and he was for nearly thirteen years, reaching a peak record of 72-1 with fifty-six knockouts. During this time he was undefeated as world lightweight champion for six years and also won the world welterweight title. At his best as lightweight champion he successfully defended the title twelve times, eleven by knockout. He fought until the age of fifty with a final career record of 103-16 (70 KOs).

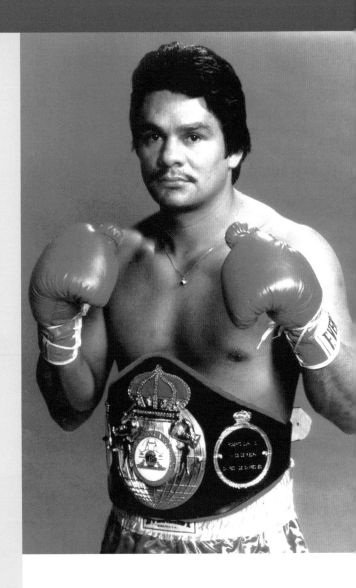

This man was the inspiration for me to succeed in boxing. He fought the best and was one of the most exciting boxers of all time.

Full Traditional English Fry-Up

DIFFICULTY LEVEL	PREPARATION TIME	COOKING TIME	SERVES
VERY EASY	5 MINUTES	10 MINUTES	4

Ingredients

8 rashers of bacon
8 pork sausages
4 slices black pudding
4 tomato halves
8 hash browns
2 slices bread
1 tin beans
4 eggs
8 slices toast
4 nice cups of tea

Method

As everybody knows, I can't even boil an egg, so what I would do is take Roberto to my local café the "Butty Box" in Hyde and let the girls do the cooking while we have a chat and a brew.

For those budding chefs among us:
Just heat the grill up and grill the bacon, sausages, and black pudding. At the same time shallow fry the hash browns and bread. Heat the beans on the stove and fry the eggs at the last minute.

Alternatives if you are on a health kick, well there are none, so just dig in to the fry-up!

19

Jane Wenham-Jones
Author and Journalist

My Hero
The Rt. Hon. Ann Widdecombe MP

My hero is definitely Ann Widdecombe. This has nothing to do with her politics and is all about the conviction she exudes. With her foghorn vowels and wonderful aura of 'Matron knows best', Ann is an abiding constant in an uncertain world: no woolly replies like 'I'm not sure' or 'I've never thought about that' for her. She is the ship of belief sailing majestically across the wish-wash of political correctness, tossing the namby-pamby aside in her wake. I particularly love her when she is making mincemeat of interviewers by disregarding their questions and only answering her own, or explaining her relationship with God. (I don't go to Church much myself, but I like other people to.) Normally known for my gobbiness, I was reduced, in the three seconds I was in her presence, to gush and blush.

I would feed her egg mayonnaise sandwiches, hand-fried crisps and a bottle of champagne (she probably doesn't drink, so all the more for me).

She is the ship of belief sailing majestically across the wish-wash of political correctness, tossing the namby-pamby aside in her wake.

Egg Mayonnaise Sandwiches and Homemade Crisps

DIFFICULTY LEVEL	PREPARATION TIME	COOKING TIME	SERVES
VERY EASY	5 MINUTES	3-5 MINUTES	2

Ingredients

2 large potatoes
2 eggs
4 slices thick bread (preferably wholemeal bread un-sliced from your local bakers)
50g butter
1 small bunch basil
2 tbsp mayonnaise
salt
black pepper

Method

1 Preheat deep fat fryer to 190C / 375F.

2 Put a small saucepan of water on to boil.

3 Peel and thinly slice the potatoes, preferably with a mandolin.

4 Put the eggs into the water and boil for 3–5 minutes, depending on how well you like your eggs cooked.

5 Deep-fry your crisps and sprinkle with salt and black pepper.

6 Chop basil and add to a bowl with the mayonnaise, salt, pepper and grate the eggs into the bowl.

7 Slice the bread and spread with butter and top with egg mixture.

8 Serve with the homemade crisps. Can be garnished with tomatoes.

My Hero
Sgt George Henry Murray

I'd cook this for my dad, my hero from as early as I can remember. A big man with a bigger heart, sadly no longer with us, he has moved on to keep things shipshape and Bristol fashion behind the pearly gates. If I had one wish, I'd sit down to dinner and a few beers with him again and 'spin dits' in true military fashion.

A Cavalry man, he started in the 13th/18th, Queen Mary's Own, Royal Hussars – 'The Lillywhites' back in the 1940s when the regiment even had a few horses. He never did like horses much after that. He moved on to tanks and armoured cars for twenty-two years of service in Germany, North Africa and Malaya (where he carelessly caught a bullet).

Do your best at everything ('if it's not worth doing properly, don't do it at all!'); admit your inevitable mistakes; help your mates out when you can; always keep your word; treat others as you hope they'll treat you: the cornerstones of his philosophy, which have served me well. The world would be a much better place if everyone held the same ideals.

The Hungry Man's Chilli Tortillas

DIFFICULTY LEVEL	PREPARATION TIME	COOKING TIME	SERVES
EASY	25-30 MINUTES	15 MINUTES	5

Serves at least 5 hungry Matelots at Gannet Search and Rescue Flight (a lot in other words!)

The Hungry Man's Chilli Tortillas

Ingredients

Sauce:
800g tomatoes
2 large red onions
2 sweet red peppers
1 fresh red chilli

Guacamole:
4 large, ripe avocado pears
½ onion
3 cloves garlic
juice of ½ lemon
olive oil

Chilli:
2 tsp chilli powder
2 large onions
½ bulb garlic
1.6 kg lean minced beef
2x400g tins chopped tomatoes
1 tube tomato puree
2x400g tins kidney beans
chilli sauce
fresh red chilli

To serve:
large tub natural Greek yoghurt
finely sliced iceberg lettuce
sliced fresh tomato, cucumber and chilli
grated mature cheddar cheese
10 flour tortillas-your choice of plain, seeded or garlic

Method

1 If possible, prepare the sauce the previous day. Cut the tomatoes, onion and peppers into cubes and put in a bowl. Add finely diced chilli and season. Add garlic if you like it. Cover and keep in the fridge.

2 For the guacamole, mash the flesh of the avocados in a bowl. Finely chop the onion, crush the garlic and add to the avocado. Stir in the lemon juice and enough olive oil to make a glossy paste; then season well with salt and pepper. Cover and keep in the fridge

3 Heat the olive oil in a large saucepan, cook the chilli powder in it for a minute or so (add more powder for a hotter chilli).

4 Dice one onion finely, the other coarsely, and add, cook for 5 minutes or so until they soften. Crush the garlic, add and cook for 2 minutes, add the mince and cook, stirring constantly, until the mince browns. This takes 5–10 minutes.

5 Add the chopped tomatoes and tomato puree. Stir thoroughly to combine. Bring to the boil, then gently simmer.

6 Stir the drained and washed kidney beans into the mixture.

7 Add sliced fresh red chilli and chilli sauce to taste. My favourite is a "siracha" sauce from Thailand ("Healthy Boy" brand!!) which adds heat and flavour but also a slight underlying sweetness which I like.

8 Simmer for a further 10 minutes and season. The chilli is now ready to be served.

9 Just before serving, warm the tortillas in the microwave or oven. Put the accompaniments into individual dishes on the table so everyone can choose their own combination of fillings for the tortillas.

In time you will probably want more and more heat. Increase the amount of chilli powder at the start or find a hotter variety, add more or hotter chilli sauce and fresh chilli. You can even add fresh chilli to the guacamole and yoghurt if you so wish.

LIEUTENANT COMMANDER
TANK MURRAY

I'm getting a bit old, am a bit fat and bear an unfortunate resemblance, so I'm told, to Antony Worrall Thompson (but then all bearded fat ginger blokes probably look similar) which may have something to do with why I like cooking and was so keen to support this book.

I've been in the Fleet Air Arm 22½ years and have 11½ to go. I'm coming to the end of three and a bit years as a pilot on Gannet Search and Rescue (SAR) Flight up in bonnie Scotland and have just passed 6000 flying hours, nearly all in the venerable Sea King.

But what have been the highs and lows of my career? Well I guess we should look at the letters I have received from the great and the good throughout to get an idea. I have an Admiral's displeasure for crashing an RAF Metro through 15 feet of a farmer's brick wall and his front room along with another for blowing up the wardroom on a Taranto Night. Combine this with a Captain's Logging for having a failure of vertical hold on my mess kit trousers during a Top Table Dinner in the Senior Rates Mess along with many, many "interviews" with various Commanding Officers, most of which did not involve coffee, and you're getting an idea of where I start from.

On the up side I have had a couple of well-dones, have had my articles published in the Fleet Air Arm's Flight Safety Magazine Cockpit several times, have been written up for but not received a few awards and was given a Green Endorsement last year for flying away from the side of a mountain during a rescue when the tail rotor suddenly lost authority in a downdraught and the aircraft span wildly out of control. I have over a thousand deck landings on just about every type of ship and have been most of the way around the world, courtesy of Her Majesty. I've also spent some time in both Iraq and, more recently, Afghanistan, a place where you'd not expect to find an old Anti-Submarine warrior.

Flying with the Royal Navy is still an absolute thrill and everyone knows I like nothing better than strapping a Sea King to my backside and taking her around the mountains, or just about anywhere else I can find an excuse to go; not every serviceman can say he has a 72 foot chopper that he can keep up for 5 hours!!

I've been shot at at least once, scared stupid on several occasions, nearly died a couple of times and have had nearly every malfunction in the book including engine fires and total losses of the main gearbox oil so have spent many an hour in various locations (usually pubs, if I could find one) waiting for the engineers to come and rescue me.

Jonny Wilkinson MBE
England and Newcastle Rugby Star

My Hero
Walter Payton

Everyone has heroes. As a sports-mad kid, it was natural that mine would be sportsmen.

One of my all-time heroes is Walter Payton, the dynamic Chicago Bears running back, who seemed to spend every weekend defying gravity to leap over defences or run straight through them for improbable touchdowns. Payton held the NFL's rushing record for eighteen years. He broke it in 1984 and when he retired after the 1987 season he had extended it to 16,726 yards. That's almost ten miles through some seriously heavy traffic. They called him Sweetness but there wasn't much sweet about running into him. He was five feet ten inches of pure power.

He wasn't the quickest running back around, but he was incredibly destructive. It wasn't all bang, crash, wallop, though – his footwork was fantastic too. What a centre he would have made if he had been introduced to rugby instead of gridiron.

Despite all the contact, he only missed one game in thirteen seasons for the Bears, which is an incredible record of durability in a sport like American football. And he wasn't just consistent, he was consistently brilliant. He was held in such

high esteem by the Bears that when he retired they retired his No. 34 jersey as well.

My recipe for Walter would consist of good, healthy food that would drive him towards finding his best and finding out what he was capable of.

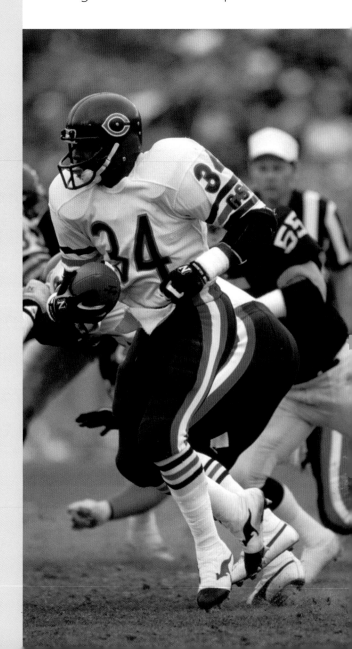

Spicy Chicken with Almonds and Apricots Pitta Pocket

Ingredients

1 large or 2 small pitta pockets
1 tbsp very low fat mayonnaise
1 tbsp low fat plain bio yoghurt
½ tbsp curry paste or powder
75–110g cooked chicken (add more to increase protein intake)
4 ready to eat dried apricots
2 spring onions
1 tbsp flaked almonds or pine nuts

DIFFICULTY LEVEL	PREPARATION TIME	COOKING TIME	SERVES
VERY EASY	10 MINUTES	10-15 MINUTES	1

Inside Knowledge

Use any left over chicken for this. Don't miss out the apricots as they go well with the spices and nuts, as well as being a good source of iron.

Chicken is a good low fat protein that is required for muscle growth and repair.

Yoghurt contains beneficial bacteria for the maintenance of the intestinal tract.

Method

1 Heat the pitta bread in the microwave for 15 seconds, using a sharp knife cut around 1 cm from the edge along the pitta to open it, pull it open and set aside.

2 Mix the mayonnaise, yoghurt and curry paste or powder in a bowl until well combined.

3 Cut the chicken, spring onion and apricot into small pieces.

4 Put them in with the curry sauce and add the almonds or pine nuts. Mix well to completely coat with the sauce.

5 Fill the pitta pocket and serve with a large salad to give extra vitamins and minerals.

Captain Chris Underhill MBE
Quartermaster, 14 Geographic Squadron Royal Engineers

My Hero
Sir Barnes Wallis CBE

He was a visionary British scientist, engineer and inventor who produced some of the most famous and ingenious inventions of the Second World War. Best known for inventing the 'Dambusters' bouncing bomb, he was also engaged in a number of ingenious inventions that were decades ahead of their time.

When WWII was declared, Barnes Wallis asked himself what he could do, as an engineer and aircraft designer, to shorten the war. His work on a variety of military projects, while impossible to measure in isolation, certainly did shorten the war. His tenacity and the quality of his engineering saw his plans, described as 'mad', 'ridiculous' and 'implausible', come to fruition and his special weapons operate exactly as he had calculated.

Applying his revolutionary geodetic principals, he revised the design of the Wellesley and the Wellington bomber aircraft, enabling it to carry double the required load and over twice the distance specified on the initial contract.

Wallis turned to developing huge bombs, the Tallboy (six tonnes) and next the Grand Slam (ten tonnes) deep-penetration earthquake bombs.

Used against targets such as V1 rocket launch sites and submarine pens, as well as Germany's largest battleship, the Tirpitz, these bombs were the forerunners of today's bunker-busting bomb

Later, Wallis did much to develop the 'swing-wing', or variable-geometry, aircraft. Some of his ideas were later used in the F-111 aircraft.

My father often met Barnes Wallis in the mid 1970s and described him as a compassionate man who emphasised that all his inventions were intended to limit the loss of life and ultimately to shorten the war.

Sir Barnes Wallis was an engineering genius, and for his dedication to quality and dogged determination he is my hero.

Dr Barnes Wallis (HU 92134) by permission of the Imperial War Museum

Greek-style Burgers

Ingredients

450g minced beef
1 tbsp sun-dried tomato paste
2 tsp dried oregano
50g feta cheese
1 egg
1 red onion
½ iceberg lettuce
2 tomatoes
4 wholemeal rolls

Method

1 In a large bowl, mix the mince, tomato paste, oregano and crumbled feta cheese. Season this mix well with salt and pepper.

2 Whisk the egg up and add to the mince, a little at a time to ensure the mixture binds together.

3 Divide the mixture evenly into four and shape into patties.

4 Chill the burgers in the fridge while you get the salad ready.

5 Slice the tomatoes and onion thinly, slice the lettuce, wash thoroughly and dry.

6 Put the burgers under a hot grill for approx 4–5 minutes each side, until brown and thoroughly cooked.

7 Lightly toast the rolls and serve the burger topped with the lettuce, tomato and onion. Eat immediately.

DIFFICULTY LEVEL	PREPARATION TIME	COOKING TIME	SERVES
EASY	15 MINUTES	10 MINUTES	4

My Hero

Barry Sheene MBE

My hero is Barry Sheene MBE. Barry was the British Motorcycling 125cc Champion aged just twenty years old. Despite two life-threatening crashes, he went on to successfully win the World 500cc Championship twice in 1976 and 1977. Apart from my dad Albert, Barry is the main reason that I took up motorcycling. From an early age I used to watch Barry racing on TV. I was always going out on the back of my dad's motorbike and wanting to be able to drive it myself. I received my first motorbike on my sixteenth birthday and still ride motorcycles with my dad to this day. You cannot beat the thrill factor and freedom of the roads, speeding along as if you did not have a care in the world. As a serviceman I can associate with Barry, as his ethics were to work hard and to play hard. Barry was a sporting legend who will never be forgotten.

'Nutter' not a Chicken

Ingredients

Dressing:
3 tbsp olive oil
1 tbsp clear honey
1 tbsp balsamic vinegar

Salad:
2 ripe pears
6 cherry tomatoes
50g pine nuts
100g Italian salad leaves
2 chicken breasts
100g stilton cheese

Method

1 First make the dressing by combining all the ingredients together, whisking well until they thicken, taste and season with salt and pepper to your liking, set aside, keeping at room temperature so the oil doesn't set.

2 Dice the pears into a small cubes, about 1cm square, and cut the cherry tomatoes into quarters, set aside.

3 Heat a frying pan with no oil and toast the pine nuts, keeping them moving, until they turn golden brown, add to the pears and tomatoes, toss the salad leaves into the mixture.

4 Cook the chicken breasts in a griddle pan (or a frying pan if you do not have a griddle) over a medium heat, seasoning well with salt and pepper on both sides, until the chicken is cooked through, remove from the heat.

5 Working quickly, slice the chicken and add to the salad with the dressing, toss thoroughly.

6 Divide the salad between two plates and crumble the stilton over the salad before serving.

'Nutter' not a Chicken

DIFFICULTY LEVEL	PREPARATION TIME	COOKING TIME	SERVES
EASY	10 MINUTES	10 MINUTES	2

My Hero
Barack Obama

Heroes come in all shapes and sizes. Sometimes they can be part of a fantasy, like that of a comic hero, although I wonder if that's got something to do with wanting to escape the world we live in as children.

As adults we are constantly looking for new heroes, and quite often they turn out to be sporting ones. Perhaps because we realise that our time has passed or our joints are just too old and bellies too fat. Who cares anyway? I could never score a goal with such aplomb as Thierry Henry, Wayne Rooney or the brilliant Catalan left-winger Messi.

But my hero is not a sportsman; he's a politician who has become the most powerful man in the world: Barack Obama, the 44th President of the United States of America, who just happens to be Afro-American. I honestly never expected to witness this in my lifetime, but already like many others, regardless of colour, race or religion, I am excited about the change and praying that my new hero will create a better world for all of our children.

Herby Couscous Salad
with Hot Paprika Chicken and Cucumber Mint Yoghurt Dressing

Ingredients

Dressing:
½ cucumber
150g pot natural yoghurt
1 tbsp chopped fresh mint
salt

Salad:
250g couscous soaked in 400ml hot chicken stock
½ pomegranate
85g ready-to-eat dried apricots
40g pistachio nuts
4 spring onions, finely chopped
2 tbsp chopped mint
2 tbsp chopped flat leaf parsley
juice of 1 lemon

Chicken:
4 chicken breasts
1 tbsp hot paprika
juice of ½ lemon
1 tsp olive oil
salt and freshly ground black pepper

DIFFICULTY LEVEL	PREPARATION TIME	COOKING TIME	SERVES
EASY	15 MINUTES	10 MINUTES	4

Herby Couscous Salad
with Hot Paprika Chicken and Cucumber Mint Yoghurt Dressing

Method

1 Prepare the dressing first: cut the cucumber in half lengthways and scrape out the seeds using a teaspoon. Coarsely grate half of the cucumber, keep the other half for the salad, sprinkle with a little salt and place in a sieve over a bowl to drain for one hour. Squeeze out any excess moisture from the cucumber, add the natural yoghurt and chopped mint.

2 Cover and chill until needed.

3 Prepare the couscous, cover and set aside.

4 Pick out the seeds from the pomegranate, removing all the pith. Roughly chop the apricots and pistachios. Finely dice the de-seeded cucumber. Mix the pomegranate seeds, apricots, pistachios and cucumber into the couscous. Add the chopped herbs and lemon juice and season well.

5 In a small bowl mix the paprika, lemon juice and oil and rub over the slashed chicken breasts season with salt and pepper. Grill under a medium grill for 6–7 minutes per side until cooked through (alternatively cook in the microwave on the grill or combi setting at 180w for 10–11 minutes until cooked through). Rest for 2 minutes before slicing each breast on the diagonal into six slices.

6 Divide the couscous between 4 plates, top with chicken and serve with the yoghurt dressing on the side.

7 Serve with warm Mediterranean flat breads.

If you can't find fresh pomegranate use dried cherries.

Paula Wilcox
Actress

My Hero
Emmeline Pankhurst

Emmeline Pankhurst would get my vote as my hero. Born in Manchester, she campaigned for equal voting rights for women, in which she was ultimately successful.

Emmeline died on 14 June 1928, shortly after women were granted equal voting rights with men (at twenty-one years old).

It's appalling that so many women don't bother to vote today. I think life for us all might be very different if they did.

Pan-fried Halloumi

Ingredients

250g halloumi
6 tbsp olive oil
6 tbsp balsamic vinegar
150–200g rocket

DIFFICULTY LEVEL	PREPARATION TIME	COOKING TIME	SERVES
EASY	5 MINUTES	5 MINUTES	4

Method

1 Carefully slice the halloumi into 1cm-thick slabs.

2 Heat the oil and vinegar in a pan, mix as much as possible.

3 When the contents of the pan are hot, add the halloumi. Fry for about 5 minutes, until the edges are nicely golden.

4 Remove from the pan and lie on a bed of rocket leaves, 2 per person.

5 Lightly drizzle a little balsamic vinegar over the dish.

Halloumi can make a tasty alternative to meat for vegetarians. It's also great to barbeque on skewers, as it doesn't melt!

vegetarian

Red Pea Soup • Spicy Lentil Curry • Roasted Vegetable
• Stuffed Flat Field Mushrooms • Goats Cheese and F
• Jamacian Red Pea Soup • Spicy Lentil Curry • Roaste
Tarte Tatin • Stuffed Flat Field Mushrooms • Goats Ch
Onion Tart • Jamacian Red Pea Soup • Spicy Lentil Curr
Vegetable Tarte Tatin • Stuffed Flat Field Mushrooms •
eese and Red Onion Tart • Jamacian Red Pea Soup • Sp
rry • Roasted Vegetable Tarte Tatin • Stuffed Flat Field
ms • Goats Cheese and Red Onion Tart • Jamacian Red
icy Lentil Curry • Roasted Vegetable Tarte Tatin • Stuffe

Aisleyne
Businesswoman and Fashion Designer

My Hero
Little Venice

Venice is the daughter of one of my best friends. Venice was diagnosed at fifteen months with neuroblastoma, an extremely rare type of children's cancer. Her mother was told Venice had a twenty per cent chance of living if the treatment was even successful. She then had six sessions of intensive chemotherapy and after each session she was knocked down with terrible infections.

One evening during this time period Venice crashed; all her organs started to shut down, and the consultant told her mum that she was not going to make it. Her mother told the consultant that he was wrong and that Venice would live. The next morning she turned the corner. Love kept her alive; even the consultant said so. Once Venice had recovered sufficiently, she had to have major abdominal surgery from which she was given only a fifty-fifty chance of surviving, dropping her overall survival expectancy ten per cent. The operation lasted twelve and a half hours, during which they had to remove the tumour that had wrapped itself around her artery and spine. Venice then had radiotherapy for six months and oral chemo after that.

Love kept her alive; even the consultant said so.

Venice is now seven years old and the most beautiful, eloquent, kind-natured and free-spirited little girl I have ever known. The only evidence of what she has been through is her extraordinary outlook on life. One example of this is when she came home from school and told her mum she was being bullied, but that it was 'OK, because she had come to a conclusion about it, she realised that it was his fault, not hers, and that she had already forgiven him'. What a lesson to learn from one so young.

Jamaican Red Pea Soup with Dumplings

DIFFICULTY LEVEL	PREPARATION TIME	COOKING TIME	SERVES
MODERATE	45 MINUTES	2 HOURS	4

Ingredients

450g self-raising flour
2 tsp caster sugar
½ tsp salt
300ml warm milk
230g red peas, red kidney beans or gungo peas
500ml water
250ml coconut milk
2 bay leaves
6 pimento grains or ½ tsp Jamaican allspice
2 whole hot peppers
1 onion
4 cloves garlic
2 carrots
2 potatoes
225g yellow yams
1 small sweet potato
2 scallions or spring onions
2 sprigs fresh thyme

Method

1 In a large bowl, mix the flour, sugar and salt together.

2 Pour in the milk a little at a time, mixing with a wooden spoon until it is doughy.

3 Divide the dough into 8 equal balls.

4 When rolled, flatten slightly.

5 Deep fry on a medium heat, till golden brown (about 12 minutes).

6 If you cook them too high, they will still be doughy in the centre (so maybe test one first).

7 Now for the soup: wash the peas or beans and soak for a few hours or overnight.

8 Add 500ml of water to the soaked peas or beans, add coconut milk, bay leaves and pimento grains and cook on a low heat for about 2 hours, until the peas/beans are tender.

9 Chop one pepper and leave one whole.

10 Chop the onion, dice the carrots, potatoes, yams, sweet potato, and scallions.

11 Add half of the onion and all diced vegetables to the soup, as well as the peppers and 2 whole garlic cloves and cook for another 20 minutes.

12 Chop one twig of thyme and leave one whole.

13 Add the rest of the onion, 2 chopped garlic cloves and the thyme.

14 Puree half of the soup to thicken and serve with the dumplings.

This is a very thick soup more like a stew, very good for the winter.

Captain Dave Rigg MC
Royal Engineer

My Hero
Harry Patch

Our last remaining veteran of
the trenches

Harry Patch, our last remaining veteran
of the trenches, is a national hero and
embodies the sacrifice made by thousands
of British troops who fought on the
Western Front in the First World War. His
reputation as the last fighting Tommy
has been well documented in the media,
but it took him more than eighty years to
break his silence. It's a testament to the
horrific experience he went through.

He is my hero for his humility, compassion,
sense of duty and for simply being a good
all-round bloke. I hope he likes lentils!

Spicy Lentil Curry
Ingredients

1 large onion
2 cloves garlic
1cm-piece fresh ginger
2 red chillies
curry paste or powder (mild 10g, hot 40g)
1 large potato
100g lentils
2 tomatoes
500ml stock, chicken or vegetable
natural yoghurt (to taste)
coriander, chopped (to taste)

Method

1 Finely dice the onion and crush the garlic.
Peel and grate the ginger and chop the
chillies into small pieces. Lightly fry all these
ingredients for a few minutes to soften and
release the flavours, stir in the curry paste or
powder and fry for a few minutes more.

2 Meanwhile, peel and cut the potato into
cubes, add the potato and lentils, stir and
cook for a few minutes, reducing the heat
if it starts to burn. Cut up the tomatoes and
add to the pan, stir.

3 Pour over the stock, stir and bring to the
boil. Reduce the heat and cover, simmering
for about 45 minutes or until lentils and
potato are soft.

4 When ready, taste and season with salt and
pepper. If needed, stir in some yoghurt and
coriander.

Serve immediately with rice.

Spicy Lentil Curry

DIFFICULTY LEVEL	PREPARATION TIME	COOKING TIME	SERVES
VERY EASY	10 MINUTES	50 MINUTES	2

CAPTAIN
DAVE RIGG MC RE

On 15th January 2007 the IX Battle Group, 3 Commando Brigade, attacked a major Taliban stronghold, Jugroom Fort, south of Garmsir in southern Helmand province and met ferocious Taliban fire from all sides. Almost immediately the Marines began to sustain serious casualties and they were forced to regroup. When they discovered Lance Corporal (LCpl) Ford was missing a plan was hatched to fly back into the Fort sitting on the wings of two Apache helicopters to find their comrade. This unique rescue mission attempt was led by Captain Dave Rigg:

Volunteering was the easy part. When the Commanding Officer accepted my offer and I was left with a moment to contemplate what it was that we were about to undertake, I felt extremely uneasy. I gathered my body armour and weapon, went outside to get some air and began to formulate a plan. The odds were stacked against us. The enemy were dug in, awaiting our return and reinforcements were streaming in from the south.

Before long I was joined by the three men that were to accompany me on our way back to Jugroom Fort. Regimental

Without a question or a moment's hesitation, the two young Marines turned and strode towards the waiting helicopters …

Sergeant Major (RSM) Hearne provided us with some much needed steadfastness, but the other two were still unaware of what it was that they had volunteered to do. Marine Robinson was 24, he was the signaller in the Battle Group HQ. 19-year-old Marine Fraser-Perry had just woken up and was making himself a hot wet when his Company 2IC asked for a volunteer. A day earlier he had been discussing various mortgage arrangements with LCpl Ford. Ten minutes later he would be perched on the side of an Apache attack helicopter and flying into a Taliban fort to recover LCpl Ford's body.

I explained the plan. Minimising the time on the ground was vital. Fraser-Perry and I were to board one Apache while the RSM and Robertson were to take the other one.

On touching down Fraser-Perry and I were to recover the fallen Marine while the other two were to provide covering fire as necessary. Another two Apaches would provide suppressive fire.

This was a tactic that had never been tried before, the details were scant and there was no contingency plan. I tried to maintain an air of confidence, to suppress my growing doubt.

Without a question or a moment's hesitation, the two young Marines turned and strode towards the waiting helicopters …

The mission was a success. All four men returned safely; with the body of their fallen comrade.

Simon Weston OBE
Former Welsh Guardsman

My Hero
Dr Sir Archibald McIndoe

My hero would be Dr Sir Archibald McIndoe. Sir Archibald was a pioneering New Zealand plastic surgeon who worked for the Royal Air Force during World War II. He greatly improved the treatment and rehabilitation of badly burned aircrew.

His important work included the development of the walking-stalk skin graft and the discovery that immersion in saline promoted healing as well as improving survival rates for victims with extensive burns. Sir Archibald sadly passed away in 1960, but if he were alive today I would cook him a delicious roasted vegetable tarte tatin.

Roasted Vegetable Tarte Tatin with a Caramelized Red Onion and Apple Chutney

Ingredients

2 cloves garlic
4 tbsp oil
1 green pepper
1 yellow pepper
1 red pepper
4–6 mushrooms
1 courgette
500g ready-made puff pastry
1 tbsp honey
6 cooking apples
2 red onions
2 tbsp brown sugar
4 tbsp water
4 tbsp white wine vinegar

DIFFICULTY LEVEL	PREPARATION TIME	COOKING TIME	SERVES
EASY	15-20 MINUTES	35 MINUTES	4

Method

1 Peel and finely chop the garlic, add to half of the oil.

2 Cut up all the vegetables, quite rustically, into a large dice.

3 Lay the vegetables in a tin and add the garlic oil and mix.

4 Roast in a moderate oven for 15 minutes.

5 While the vegetables are in the oven, cut the pastry into four equal sizes.

Roasted Vegetable Tarte Tatin
with a Caramelized Red Onion and Apple Chutney

6 Roll out to desired size or shape (you can make a big one and cut up).

7 Grease suitable tin or earthenware dish and layer with the cooked vegetables.

8 Brush the pastry with honey and lay honey side down onto the vegetables.

9 Press down and bake in a moderate oven for 10–15 minutes.

10 While the tarte tatin is cooking, slice the onions thinly, peel and dice the apples.

11 Seal the onions in the other half of the oil until soft and then add the apples, water, sugar and vinegar. Cook until the apples are soft (you may need more water).

12 This can be served either hot or cold.

Tony Blair
Former Prime Minister

My Hero
Mahatma Gandhi

Einstein said of Gandhi: "Future generations will scarce believe that such a one as this ever in flesh and blood walked upon this earth." Of course, Gandhi made misjudgements and mistakes. But he has endured as one of those iconic individuals who shape how we think about society and about ourselves.

A Hindu and deeply rooted within the culture of India, he nonetheless transcended boundaries of racial and religious identity.

Gandhi taught that the greatest risk to humanity lay within what he identified as the Seven Social Sins: "Wealth without Work, Worship without Sacrifice, Politics without Principle, Pleasure without Conscience, Knowledge without Character, Commerce without Morality and Science without Humanity".

Within these elegant and sparing mantras I believe that we can find timeless guidance, whatever our own faith or lack of it.

Through his teaching, and his life, Gandhi embodied his creed that "We must become the change we want to see in the world."

He embodied these beliefs throughout his life, resisting discrimination in South Africa, renouncing his life of material comfort and refusing to renounce his respect for all the great faiths, treating all faiths equally.

In an increasingly globalised world we all need to develop greater respect for those who differ from us, and find what unites us in terms of common values. Gandhi's Seven Social Sins point to values around which people of any faith or of none can unite.

He believed that we are all children of God, and preached tolerance for all men, an ideal which makes him my personal hero.

Stuffed Flat Field Mushrooms
with a Tomato and Tarragon Sauce

Ingredients

3 large flat field mushrooms
1 yellow pepper
1 green pepper
1 beef tomato
2 small tomatoes
selection of shelled nuts
olive oil

For the sauce:
½ onion
400g tin tomatoes
2 tbsp tomato puree
few sprigs tarragon
salt and pepper

Method

1 Peel the mushrooms and brush lightly with olive oil.

2 Cut the four sides of the peppers and roast for 5 minutes, peel off skin and cut into a circle about the same size as the mushroom.

3 Finely chop the nuts and small tomatoes and add salt and pepper, then fill two of the flat field mushrooms.

4 Slice the beef tomato and layer on top of the stuffed mushroom, add a circle of pepper, then another mushroom then tomato then another pepper and then finish with mushroom.

5 Place on a baking tray and put a cocktail stick through the middle to hold in place.

6 Bake in a medium oven for about 5–10 minutes.

7 For the sauce, finely chop the onion and cook in a little olive oil for 2–3 minutes.

8 Whiz the tinned tomatoes in a food processor for a few seconds and add to the onions with the tomato puree.

9 When this has cooked out season and finish with some chopped tarragon.

This is good for a light lunch.

DIFFICULTY LEVEL	PREPARATION TIME	COOKING TIME	SERVES
EASY	10 MINUTES	10 MINUTES	2

My Hero
Nelson Mandela

A hero of both this century and the last must be Nelson Mandela. After twenty-seven years in prison, he remains an incredibly dignified man who continues to devote his life to his ideals of what is fair and right. His leadership in advocating forgiveness through reconciliation is admired and respected throughout the world. He was awarded the Nobel Peace Prize in 1993 (jointly with F.W. de Klerk), which was justly deserved and long overdue. I cannot think of anyone who deserves the accolade 'Hero' more than this man.

Goats Cheese and Red Onion Tart on Mixed Leaves with a Balsamic Reduction

Ingredients

Pastry:
200g plain flour
1 tsp salt
100g chilled butter
water to bind

Filling:
1 red onion
2 eggs
200ml cream
½ tsp fresh thyme
100g goats cheese
100ml dark balsamic vinegar
mixed salad leaves to serve, such as lollo rosso, curly endive and rocket

Method

1 Sift the flour into a large bowl, add the salt and rub the cubed butter in with your fingertips until the mixture resembles fine breadcrumbs. Gradually add cold water to form a firm ball of dough, and refrigerate for an hour.

2 Knead the dough a little and roll out to 1cm thickness, cut out two circles and line two mini flan tins. Line with baking paper and cover with baking beans, partially bake for ten minutes at 200C / 400F / Gas Mark 6. Remove and put on a baking sheet.

3 Cook the thinly sliced onions in a little oil for 5 minutes until soft. Lay them in the pastry cases, then break the goat's cheese up into ½ inch pieces and divide between the two.

Goats Cheese and Red Onion Tart
on Mixed Leaves with a Balsamic Reduction

DIFFICULTY LEVEL	PREPARATION TIME	COOKING TIME	SERVES
EASY	20 MINUTES PLUS CHILLING TIME	10–15 MINUTES	4

4 Whisk the eggs, then add cream and season well with salt, pepper and thyme. Pour into the cases, topping them up inside the oven to avoid spillage.

5 Bake at 160C / 300F / Gas Mark 3 for 15–20 minutes, until just set.

6 Boil the balsamic vinegar rapidly until reduced in volume and syrupy, allow to cool.

7 If the tarts have not browned, finish them off under a hot grill or a kitchen blowtorch.

8 Serve the warm tarts on a base of salad leaves, drizzled with the balsamic reduction.

49

seafood

ston Non-Clam Chowder • Salmon Potato and Pasta B
ral's Pie • Fresh Sea Bass with a delicate Lemon Risotto
lfrezi Pittas • Vietnamese Rice Paper Roll with Portland
edgeree • Fresh Tagliatelle with Leek and Prawns • Thai
wn Curry • Fish Lovers' Lasagne • Baked Salmon with Le
ollandaise • Prawn with Tomato and Feta • Panga Tand
ston Non-Clam Chowder • Salmon Potato and Pasta B
ral's Pie • Fresh Sea Bass with a delicate Lemon Risotto
lfrezi Pittas • Vietnamese Rice Paper Roll with Portland
edgeree • Fresh Tagliatelle with Leek and Prawns • Thai

My Hero
Roy Webb

Everyone seems to assume heroes have to have done one or more spectacular, dramatic things to inspire men and women to follow them. For me, heroes are the people around us who make the world a better place by their very presence; despite whatever personal adversity they are going through. Take my granddad for instance: he was in a reserved trade throughout the war and so never went near a battlefield. But he was a mild-mannered grafter for every day that he worked, and every day after that. You'd always find him in a cheery mood, and he would give the time of day to anyone. He was generous to a fault, would go to the end of the earth for my sister and me and was always courteous, patient, kind and hilariously funny – always ready with a joke.

Heroes are those who leave an indelible mark on a person. You won't find Royston Webb listed in any history textbooks, but I wouldn't have swapped him for anyone. I only hope I can emulate his many great personal qualities.

Boston Non-Clam Chowder

Ingredients

1 medium onion
1 clove garlic
2 tbsp olive oil
125ml white wine
750ml fish stock (made from stock cubes)
2 medium potatoes
200g cooked, peeled prawns
300g cooked white fish or scallops
500ml double cream
1 tbsp each chopped fresh parsley and dill

DIFFICULTY LEVEL	PREPARATION TIME	COOKING TIME	SERVES
EASY	10 MINUTES	30 MINUTES	2 AS A STARTER

Boston Non-Clam Chowder

Method

1 Cut the onion into small dice and crush the garlic. Sweat the onions in the oil until soft and translucent, add the garlic and cook for a further 2 minutes.

2 Add the wine and stock, bring to boiling point and simmer for 10 minutes to release the flavours.

3 Meanwhile, cut the potatoes into roughly 1-cm cubes and add them to the stock, cooking for a further 10 minutes.

4 While the potatoes are cooking, chop up the prawns and fish.

5 Roughly mash the potatoes in the chowder, this will thicken the soup.

6 Add the double cream, fish and prawns and bring to the boil. Simmer for a final minute to heat the fish through.

7 Taste and season the soup to your liking.

8 As a serving option, cut the top of a large crusty white roll, scoop out the soft innards. Use this as a bowl. Otherwise, serve the soup in a warm bowl and sprinkle with the dill and parsley.

NOTE: If using scallops do not cook for more than a minute, as they can go chewy.

My Hero
Sir Steve Redgrave

Steve Redgrave is an absolute legend. It's not just that he is an Olympic gold medallist in one of the toughest endurance sports, but he also stayed at the top of his game for five Olympics over a sixteen-year period. He was not just an Olympic gold medallist, but also a winner of British, European and World titles. He is such a superb role model for kids and sport in general.

Salmon, Potato & Pasta Broth
Ingredients

600g salmon fillet
350g potatoes
1 chilli
2 bunches basil
1 onion
2 cloves garlic
150g baby spinach
900ml vegetable stock
200ml white wine
200ml cream
200g thin macaroni
1 tbsp olive oil

Method

1 Cut the salmon into bite-size chunks.

2 Wash, peel and cut the potatoes into small dice.

3 Finely chop the chilli, basil and garlic.

4 Finely dice the onion.

5 Heat the oil in a pan and add the onion and cook for 1–2 minutes. Add the garlic, potatoes and chilli.

6 Add the wine and reduce slightly, then add the stock.

7 Simmer until the potatoes are almost soft, about 10 minutes.

8 In a separate pan, fully cook the macaroni in boiling water and then drain the water.

9 Wash the spinach and add to the potatoes, also add the macaroni and salmon.

10 After a few minutes, add the basil and cream.

11 Simmer for about 5 minutes or until the salmon is cooked.

Salmon, Potato and Pasta Broth

DIFFICULTY LEVEL	PREPARATION TIME	COOKING TIME	SERVES
MODERATE	20 MINUTES	25 MINUTES	4

Right Reverend Thomas Matthew Burns SM BA BD

Bishop of the Forces

My Hero
Admiral Lord Nelson

Before the Battle of Trafalgar, Nelson gathered his captains together. After briefing them thoroughly, he returned them to their ships. He never amended an existing order or issued another one after that. All he required of his men was summed up in his signal before battle: 'England expects every man to do his duty'. Every guest expects the chef to follow the recipe!

Admiral's Pie

Ingredients

400g white fish, (such as cod or haddock) skinned and boned, your fishmonger can do this
250ml milk
100g prawns
6 tbsp butter
3 tbsp flour
1 tbsp chopped fresh parsley
2 tsp grated lemon peel
650g potatoes
100g grated cheddar cheese
lemon wedges and fresh parsley to garnish

Method

1 Preheat the oven to 190C / 375F / Gas Mark 5.

2 Put the fish into a medium saucepan and season well with salt and pepper. Cover with the milk and then simmer. Cover and poach for 5 minutes or until the fish is cooked. Remove the fish using a slotted spoon and save the milk. Flake the fish into small pieces into a 1½ litre-casserole dish, adding the prawns. Set this aside.

3 Melt half the butter in a saucepan, stir in the flour and cook for 1 minute. Stirring all the time, gradually add the milk to make a smooth sauce. Add more milk from the fridge, if you need to. Simmer for 2 minutes, stirring all the time. Finally, add the parsley and lemon peel to the sauce and pour over the fish. Put this to one side but keep it warm.

4 Meanwhile, boil the potatoes in a pan of salted water until cooked. Drain and mash thoroughly, adding the remaining butter and seasoning with salt and pepper to taste. Stir in half the cheese.

Admiral's Pie

DIFFICULTY LEVEL	PREPARATION TIME	COOKING TIME	SERVES
FAIRLY EASY	45 MINUTES	1 HOUR	4

5 Put the potatoes into a piping bag with a star nozzle and pipe over the fish mix (if you do not have a piping bag, spoon the potatoes on, starting with the edges to prevent the mix falling out).

6 Sprinkle over the remaining cheese and bake the pie in the preheated oven for 20–25 minutes or until the top is golden brown.

7 Serve with your chosen vegetables and garnished with the parsley and lemons.

My Hero
Elizabeth David

Elizabeth David led a food revolution in Britain in the 1950s, paving the way for what we all accept as today's 'Modern British' cooking. In the post-Second World War period she dared to be interested in cuisine from France, Italy, Greece, the Middle East, even India, and via her recipe books she brought these 'foreign' foods to the British table, broadening our tastes and improving our diets. Today, herbs, spices, pastas, terrines, lightly cooked vegetables and colourful, fruity desserts are all considered part of our everyday dining culture. Elizabeth David led the way.

For my hero I would cook fresh seabass with a delicate lemon risotto – exactly the sort of food she liked to eat.

Seabass with a Delicate Lemon Risotto
Ingredients

Risotto:
1 medium onion
3 lemons
4 tbsp olive oil
350g rice
1 litre vegetable stock
150ml double cream
150g freshly grated Parmesan
1 packet chives

Fish:
2 lemons
6x150g sea bass fillets skin on
olive oil
salt and pepper

Method

1 Finely dice the onion, remove the rind from the lemons and save. Then squeeze the juice from the lemons into a small bowl.

2 Heat the olive oil in a large heavy-based saucepan and cook the diced onion for about 5 minutes, until it begins to soften.

3 Now, stir in the rice and heat through for one minute, until shiny and opaque.

4 Turn down the heat and add the stock and lemon juice a ladle at a time. Allow the rice to absorb the liquid before adding anymore, this should take 20–30 minutes, stirring regularly.

5 When the rice feels soft and fluffy and the texture is creamy but firm, the risotto is ready. Stir in the lemon rind, double cream, grated Parmesan. Chop the chives and add.

Sea Bass with a Delicate Lemon Risotto

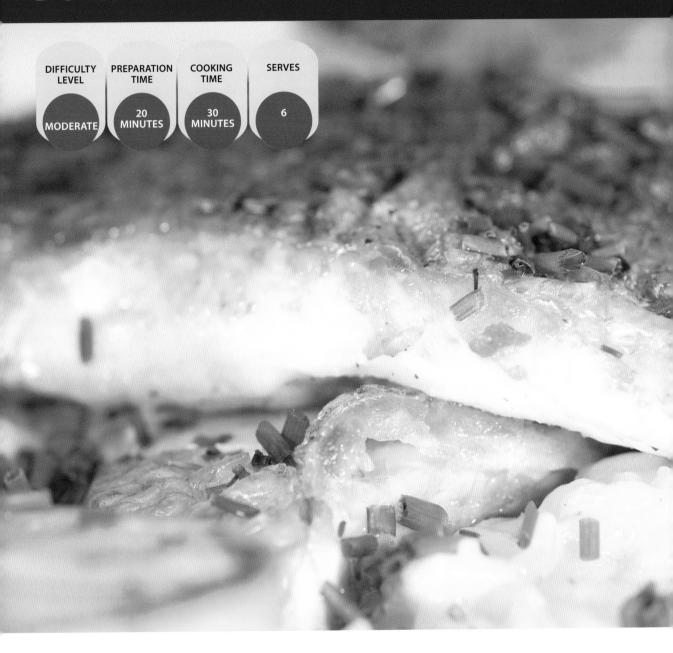

DIFFICULTY LEVEL	PREPARATION TIME	COOKING TIME	SERVES
MODERATE	20 MINUTES	30 MINUTES	6

6 For the fish: slice the ends off the lemons and cut into 3 thick slices.

7 Season the sea bass with olive oil, salt and ground black pepper. Preheat a ridged griddle pan and cook the fillets skin side down for 3–4 minutes until the skin is golden and crispy. Turn over and briefly cook the other side.

8 Smear the lemons on the griddle, alongside the fish, until caramelized.

9 Present the sea bass skin up with lemons on top and serve the risotto alongside.

Warrant Officer 2
Kieron Conlan (AQMS)
Royal Electrical and Mechanical Engineers

My Hero
Dave Grohl

Dave Grohl is my chosen hero. A multi-talented and well-respected musician, he is currently the frontman for one of the best (in my humble opinion!) rock bands of this generation, the Foo Fighters. Dave is my hero for many reasons. Personally, he is the inspiration that drove me, four years ago, to finally bite the bullet and pick up a guitar (at the age of thirty-three, mid-life crisis approaching?). What I find most fascinating about Dave Grohl is the story behind the first Foo Fighters album and the formation of the band. After the suicide of Kurt Cobain, Dave, the at this point ex-drummer of Nirvana, retired to a studio to record an album solo. This was a true solo project as he alone wrote the songs, sang, played all the instruments, got a record deal from the demo and only then formed a band to tour the album. It is this DIY, no-nonsense attitude to music that I find truly remarkable about him.

I would serve Dave my favourite dish, fish jalfrezi: a simple, quick, yet tasty meal that is very sociable to eat. Washing it down with a couple of ice cold Tiger beers, I would relish the chance to chat to Dave about his music and his own influences, and hopefully persuade him to teach me a few riffs!

Personally, he is the inspiration that drove me, four years ago, to finally bite the bullet and pick up a guitar (at the age of thirty-three, mid-life crisis approaching?).

Fish Jalfrezi Pittas

Ingredients

1 onion
1 red pepper
1 green pepper
2 cloves garlic
1 small piece ginger
1 fresh chilli
3 tbsp vegetable/olive oil
¼ tsp cumin seeds
½ tsp ground cumin
½ tsp ground coriander
½ tsp chilli powder
¼ tsp salt
400g tin tuna
¼ tsp garam masala
1 tsp lemon juice
2 tbsp chopped coriander
4 pitta breads

DIFFICULTY LEVEL	PREPARATION TIME	COOKING TIME	SERVES
EASY	30 MINUTES	8-10 MINUTES	4

Method

1 Finely chop the garlic and chilli, peel and grate the ginger and set aside.

2 Finely slice the onion and peppers.

3 Heat the oil in a wok and add the cumin seeds for 30–40 seconds until they begin to splutter.

4 Add the ground cumin, coriander, chilli powder and salt to the pan and cook for 2 minutes.

5 Add the garlic, onions and pepper and increase the heat a little. Saute for about 5 minutes.

6 Stir in the tuna, fresh chilli and grated ginger and cook for a little longer.

7 Add the garam masala, lemon juice and fresh coriander and cook through.

8 Serve in the warm pitta breads with a cucumber raita.

Sir Steve Redgrave
Five-time Olympic Gold Medal Winner

My Hero
Mark Spitz

A true Olympic hero, Mark Spitz was one of the best swimmers there ever was. He came to international fame when he won seven gold medals in the 1972 Olympics.

I remember as a sports-mad boy, watching on my parents' TV this twenty-two- year-old swimming phenomenon make history. Not only did he win seven gold medals, but he also entirely dominated the pool, breaking seven world records on the way.

After the 1972 games he retired from competitive swimming at only twenty-two years of age. If he had carried on, who knows what he could have achieved in his sport.

Both the magnitude of Mark Spitz's achievements and the manner in which he dominated that Olympic Games have been one of the major inspirations behind my sporting successes.

Baked Salmon with Lemon Hollandaise
Ingredients

2 eggs
2 tbsp lemon juice
110g butter
2 salmon darnes or fillets
25g butter

Method for the sauce (manual process):

1 Separate the eggs (as you need the yolks) and put into a bowl, add salt and pepper. Whisk in a bowl over another bowl of hot water.

2 Heat the lemon juice and add to the yolks, whisking all the time until the mixture becomes thick and pale.

3 Melt the butter and add to the egg mixture very slowly, whisking all the time.

4 This is all you need to do, now just keep the sauce over a bain marie (pan of hot water) until you need to use it.

Method for the sauce (using a food processor):

1 Separate the eggs (as you need the yolks) and put them into a food processor. Whisk on fast, heat the lemon juice in a pan and add to the eggs steadily, until mixture is pale and thick.

2 Melt the butter and add to the egg mixture steadily, while the machine is on.

3 When all the butter is added take the mixture out of the blender and place in a bain marie.

Now for the salmon: simply place onto a baking tray season and brush with butter and bake in the oven for 8–10 minutes in a pre-heated moderate oven.

Baked Salmon with Lemon Hollandaise

This is good, served with roasted new potatoes and broccoli.

DIFFICULTY LEVEL	PREPARATION TIME	COOKING TIME	SERVES
EASY	30 MINUTES	8-10 MINUTES	2

Chris Tombling

Head Chef at Mandarin Oriental Hyde Park, London

My Hero

Jeff Bland

Executive Head Chef at The Balmoral Hotel in Edinburgh

Jeff was the first Executive Chef I worked under, initially part-time job and then, after college, full time in his kitchen. He inspired me and encouraged me to get involved, giving me lots of opportunities to show him I was capable of doing the job as a commis chef. He was an example to us that if you worked hard and demonstrated your flair and enthusiasm, you could succeed and make a career of the job. Jeff is a traditionally trained chef with the enviable balance of skills rare in modern kitchens, forward-thinking with an exciting vision for modern food. He was to me a gleaming example of how an Executive Chef should be: a towering figure of knowledge and hope. He was always fair; I rarely saw him lose his temper, which is uncommon in a chef. His example has stayed with me, helping me to climb to my current position at Mandarin Oriental Hyde Park. Sometimes I wonder if he's proud that, through him, one of his fledglings has made it to this stage in his career….

Vietnamese Rice Paper Rolls with Portland Crabmeat, Raw Vegetables, Chilli and Lime Dipping Sauce

Ingredients

1 small carrot
¼ cucumber
1 head baby gem lettuce
4 lollo rosso leaves
180g white crab meat
½ lemon
½ ripe avocado
2 limes
100ml chilli syrup
4 rice papers

DIFFICULTY LEVEL	PREPARATION TIME	COOKING TIME	SERVES
MODERATE	15–20 MINUTES	NO COOKING REQUIRED	2

Method

1 Wash and peel the vegetables, cut the carrots into fine thin strips, any length but not too short.

2 Wash and pat dry the lettuce.

3 Pick the crab meat and check for any cartilage.

4 Squeeze the juice from the lemon and add to the crab, season.

5 Cut the avocado lengthwise into strips about ½cm thick.

6 Juice and zest the limes, then blanch the zest for 10 seconds and cool in icy water.

Vietnamese Rice Paper Rolls with Portland
Crabmeat, Raw Vegetables, Chilli and Lime Dipping Sauce

7 Strain the chillies out of the sauce, add the lime juice and zest to taste.

8 Get a small tray of cold water and submerge the rice paper wrappers in the water, for about one minute, until they become soft.

9 Lift them out and place on a flat surface.

10 Divide your ingredients into four, then lay them out lengthwise onto four rice papers, bringing them tightly together.

11 Fold the ends of the wrappers in, then roll the wrappers to form a thick roll.

12 Cut them in half, lay them out and serve the sauce in a small bowl to dip in.

This is a healthy, refreshing and simple dish, which has a great effect and good flavour. Ideal for a get-together in the summer with a fine glass of white wine.

My Hero
Flight Lieutenant Michelle Goodman

To my mind, a hero is someone who has carried out a courageous act. Many of my heroes have been explorers or mountaineers – from the polar explorer Apsley Cherry-Garrard to Doug Scott, a prolific and successful climber of the Himalayas. Other heroes include the men of past military actions from the daring mini-sub attack led by Lieutenant (later Rear Admiral) Basil Place VC against the Tirpitz, and Rifleman Bhanbhagta Gurung VC with his extraordinary acts of courage in Burma.

There have been many acts of courage carried out during the recent conflicts in Iraq, Afghanistan and elsewhere, though many are unrecorded and often unrewarded.

Flight Lieutenant Michelle Goodman was awarded the Distinguished Flying Cross for flying a Merlin helicopter into enemy fire in Basrah on 1 June 2007 in order to rescue a seriously wounded soldier.

Despite modern technology, a helicopter remains vulnerable to attack and it will inevitably draw fire from enemy forces. The approach to the landing zone was complex, with numerous obstructions further complicated by flying on night-vision goggles. During the approach, the helicopter was hit by enemy fire, but Michelle pushed on, undeterred. The landing zone continued to come under fire from mortars and other weapons with at least four explosions in the immediate area. Despite all this, the wounded soldier was safely evacuated and the actions of Flight Lieutenant Goodman undoubtedly saved his life.

Michelle certainly carried out a courageous act – she and her crew elected to fly into a dangerous situation in order to save the life of another person – and she is a true hero.

courtesy of Jon Enoch/The Times

Kedgeree

DIFFICULTY LEVEL	PREPARATION TIME	COOKING TIME	SERVES
EASY	20 MINUTES	20 MINUTES	2

Ingredients

300g smoked fish
1 egg
1 medium onion
50g butter
½ tsp ground coriander
½ tsp cumin
½ tsp chilli powder
4 cardamom pods
100g basmati rice
1 lemon
5 sprigs fresh coriander

Method:

1 Put the fish in a large pan and cover with cold water. Bring to the boil, then turn down the heat and simmer for 6 minutes until the fish is cooked.

2 While the fish is cooking, boil the egg for about 5 minutes.

3 Remove the fish and keep warm, but keep the liquor.

4 Peel and slice the onion and open the cardamom pods. Fry until soft, then add all the spices and cardamom pods and cook for 1 minute.

5 Wash the rice thoroughly, then add to the onion and spices. Add most of the fish cooking liquor until it just covers the rice, then leave to cook gently for 15 minutes.

6 Minutes before the rice is cooked, shell and roughly cut the egg and flake the fish.

7 Take the zest and the juice from the lemon and add to the rice with the remaining ingredients

Warrant Officer Pete Slater
RAF Warrant Officer

My Hero

Jonny Wilkinson

Of course Jonny was instrumental in England's 2003 World Cup win. But not only is he a great rugby player, he is also a fantastic ambassador for rugby and a role model for others to follow. His dedication is second to none and away from the sport he keeps a low profile, always allowing other high-profile sportsmen to take the limelight.

The Sun/NI Syndication

Fresh Tagliatelle with Leek and Prawns

Ingredients

Pasta:
500g strong bread flour
5 eggs
pinch of salt
2 tbsp olive oil

Sauce:
1 small leek
200g mushrooms
1 chilli
½ lemon
Parmesan cheese
200g king prawns
200g creme fraiche
splash of white wine
olive oil and butter for frying
salt and pepper

Method

1 First, to make the pasta, start by separating the eggs (you only need the yolks).

2 Mix and knead all the pasta ingredients together, to form a smooth silky dough.

3 Wrap in cling film and put into the fridge for half an hour.

4 Use a pasta machine to make tagliatelle, or roll out dough to thin sheet and slice into 1cm strips.

5 For the sauce, finely dice the leek and chop the mushrooms.

6 Finely chop the chilli.

7 Grate the rind from the lemon and squeeze the juice.

Fresh Tagliatelle with Leek and Prawns

DIFFICULTY LEVEL	PREPARATION TIME	COOKING TIME	SERVES
HARD	40–50 MINUTES	20–30 MINUTES	4

8 Use a peeler and remove some shavings from the Parmesan.

9 Put the olive oil and butter into a pan and fry off the leeks and chilli, until translucent.

10 Add the mushrooms and cook for 1 minute. Add the wine and reduce.

11 Add prawns and lemon and cook for 2 minutes.

12 Now, cook the pasta in boiling water and a little olive oil for 4 minutes.

13 Add the creme fraiche to the sauce and season to taste.

14 Drain the pasta and add to the sauce.

15 Put pasta into bowls and top with Parmesan cheese. Serve immediately.

My Hero
Field Marshal
The Viscount Slim

My hero is Field Marshal The Viscount Slim, regarded by many as the greatest British general of the Second World War. His career was one of selfless service and devotion to duty.

He was born into a lower-middle class family and began service life as a Territorial Private Soldier. He rose to be Chief of the Imperial General Staff, Britain's top military post, was promoted to Field Marshal and became Governor-General of Australia.

His humble background, and 'lead-from-the-front' attitude inspired his troops and gained him unreserved respect.

At a time when he had half a million troops under his command, Slim told his men, 'I have commanded every kind of formation from a section upwards to this army. I understand the British soldier because I have been one.' He believed that as an officer, he must set an example for his men: 'Officers are there to lead. As officers, you can neither eat, nor drink, nor sleep, nor even sit down until you have personally seen that your men have done these things. If you will do this for them, they will follow you to the end of the world.'

Slim was raised in Birmingham and transferred to the British Indian Army after the First World War so my meal for him would have to be Britain's most popular dish, a curry.

General Sir William Slim (D 25026) by permission of the Imperial War Museum

Thai King Prawn Curry with Thai Fragrant Rice

Ingredients

800g basmati rice
2 limes
2 stalks lemon grass
1 onion
1 tbsp chilli powder
1 tbsp ground coriander
2 bulbs garlic
1 tsp salt
1 tsp ground black pepper
4 tbsp vegetable oil
250 ml coconut cream
800g king prawns
1 cucumber
1 bunch fresh coriander

Method

1 To cook the rice: use a cup or mug to measure the rice. Put the rice into an earthenware dish. Use the mug to add equal amounts of water to the rice. Season with salt and pepper.

2 Grate the limes and put the zest to one side. Cut up the remainder of the lime and add to the rice. Pop in one stick of lemon grass, then place foil over the top of the dish and bake at 180C / 350F / Gas Mark 4 for 30–45 minutes, until the rice is soft.

3 While the rice is cooking, roughly cut the onion and the other stick of lemon grass. Put the lime zest into a food processor and blend with the onion, chilli, ground coriander, garlic, salt, black pepper, lemon grass and vegetable oil, until it has the consistency of a smooth paste. You may need a little water to help.

4 In a wok, add the coconut cream and bring to the boil. Add the ground spice mix and cook over a low heat for 10 minutes, until a film of oil appears around the edge of the pan.

5 De-shell and de-tail the prawns. Cut the cucumber length ways, de-seed and cut into moon slices. Add to the cream and cook for another 10 minutes.

6 Stir well and garnish with chopped coriander.

DIFFICULTY LEVEL	PREPARATION TIME	COOKING TIME	SERVES
MODERATE	30 MINUTES	30-45 MINUTES	4

Admiral Sir Jonathon Band KCB ADC
First Sea Lord and Chief of Naval Staff

My Hero
Admiral Sir Andrew Browne Cunningham

My hero is one of the Navy's best and most successful strategic leaders in the Second World War: Admiral Sir Andrew Browne Cunningham, Commander-in-Chief of the Mediterranean.

His personal example is exceptional; valiant and tenacious in action, staunchly loyal to his superiors, inspiring his men to great courage and remarkable achievements, despite the difficulties they faced in the campaign. Fighting both the Italian and German navies, dominating the theatre despite always operating with inferior numbers, he won some spectacular victories: Taranto in November 1940 and Cape Matapan in March 1941.

A man of flair (well-known for Grand Prix-style driving and for flicking butterballs across a banquet table with his spoon), he was an excellent delegator. He knew his men, who responded magnificently to the trust he placed in them, once proven,

Sometimes short-tempered, he demanded performance without error or hesitation, inspiring a mixture of fear and respect and achieving his aims through daring, drive and an instinct to close

and destroy the enemy at every chance – straight out of the Nelsonian mould.

The consummate war fighter, he was always looking to take the battle to the enemy, certain and decisive but never reckless. His attitude is exemplified in the evacuation of troops in Greece and Crete from German invasion in April and May 1941. Without air cover, the fleet responded magnificently to his call that the Navy must not let the Army down. Of 22,000 troops on Crete, 16,500 were rescued but three cruisers and six destroyers were sunk and a further fifteen major warships damaged. At the height of the evacuation he was told that the Navy should consider withdrawing. His response was typical Cunningham: 'It takes 3 years to build a ship, 300 years to build a tradition. We'll stay.'

If he came to dinner I would offer him Fish Lasagne, although I'd be careful to keep the butter out of his reach!

Admiral Sir Andrew Cunningham (A 9760) by permission of the Imperial War Museum

Fish Lovers' Lasagne

DIFFICULTY LEVEL	PREPARATION TIME	COOKING TIME	SERVES
MODERATE	35 MINUTES	40 MINUTES	12

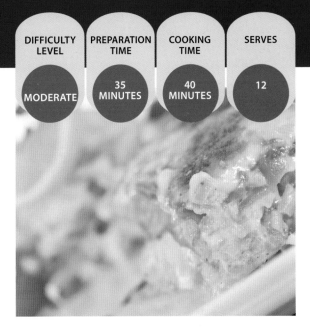

Ingredients

110g butter
110g plain flour
800ml hot milk
100ml dry sherry
1 tbsp lemon juice
225ml double cream
1 tbsp chopped parsley (fresh)
700g fennel bulb
400g leeks
4 tbsp olive oil
450g medium-sized prawns
450g scallops
450g cod fillet
1 large egg, beaten
4 tbsp lemon juice
16 lasagne sheets
3 tbsp fine, dry breadcrumbs
200g grated parmesan cheese

Method

1 Pre-heat the oven to 180C / 350F / Gas Mark 4.

2 Melt the butter and stir in the flour until smooth, cook for 3 minutes, constantly stirring. Add the milk gradually, stirring to create a smooth sauce. Add sherry and lemon juice to get the correct consistency. Cook over very low heat for 10 minutes, stirring occasionally. Remove from heat and stir in the cream, add the parsley if using, season to taste. Keep warm.

3 Wash and finely dice the fennel and leeks. Lightly fry in two tablespoons of the oil until soft, seasoning with salt and pepper.

4 Cut the prawns in half, the scallops into quarters and all the cod into a medium dice. Cook the shrimps in one tablespoon of oil over a high heat, seasoning with salt and pepper, for about 30 seconds each side. Add to the vegetable mixture.

5 Cook the scallops and cod in the remaining oil until just cooked through, (about 90 seconds) seasoning the fish with salt and pepper. Add to the shrimp mixture.

6 Whisk the egg and lemon juice together and stir into the seafood mixture.

7 Line a baking dish with a thin layer of sauce, cover with 4 lasagne sheets, spread 1/3 of fish mixture over and sprinkle with 1 tablespoon of breadcrumbs, another layer of sauce followed by about ¼ of the parmesan sprinkled on top.

8 Repeat to form 2 more layers, ending with a layer of lasagne sheets. Spread the remaining sauce over the top, ensuring the lasagne is completely covered, top with a final sprinkle of Parmesan.

9 Cover the dish with foil, bake in the middle of the oven for 30 minutes. Remove foil and bake for a further 10 minutes or until golden and bubbling. It's ready when a sharp knife goes easily through it.

10 Allow to rest for 5 minutes. Serve with a green salad.

Dame Kelly Holmes
Olympic Athlete and ex-Army Sergeant

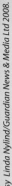

My Hero
Lord Sebastian Coe

In his phenomenal athletics career as a middle distance runner, Seb Coe won the 1500 metre gold medal at the Moscow and Los Angeles Olympic Games in 1980 and 1984, and set eight outdoor and three indoor world records. Following his retirement from athletics, he went on to become an MP, a life peer in 2000 and head of the successful London bid to host the 2012 Summer Olympics. Watching Seb compete in the Olympics was the inspiration behind my success in athletics.

Prawns with Tomato and Feta

Ingredients

2 small onions
2 cloves garlic
3 tbsp olive oil
2x400g tins chopped tomatoes
pinch of sugar
350g large peeled prawns
100g feta
3 tbsp chopped fresh parsley
handful of torn basil leaves
200g cooked rice or pasta to serve

Method

1 Finely chop the onions and crush the garlic cloves. Heat the oil in a pan and fry the onions and garlic over a low heat for 5 minutes until soft and translucent.

2 Next, add the tomatoes and a good pinch of sugar and simmer the mixture for 5 minutes.

3 Throw in the prawns, season well with salt and freshly ground black pepper and gently cook for 5 minutes, ensuring the prawns are cooked.

4 Take the mixture off the heat and stir in the crumbled feta and herbs.

5 Serve immediately over the piping hot pasta or rice.

6 Enjoy.

Prawns with Tomato and Feta

DIFFICULTY LEVEL	PREPARATION TIME	COOKING TIME	SERVES
VERY EASY	10 MINUTES	20 MINUTES	4

Edward Fox
Actor

courtesy of The Sun/NI Syndication

My Hero
Steve Thoburn
'The Metric Martyr'

Steve Thoburn became known affectionately as the 'Metric Martyr' when he was the first person to be prosecuted under the Metric Regulations for 'selling a pound of bananas'. Steve became the people's champion for his courage in standing up for his customers' right to buy their fruit and vegetables in imperial measures. He was a good and brave man, tragically dying of a heart attack at just thirty-nine. Steve received massive support from across the country and there were thousands at his funeral. His plain-speaking honesty and his humour touched many and his determination to uphold the purest of principles elevated him to iconic status amongst the patriotic British public.

Panga Tandoori
Ingredients
2 cloves garlic
1 tsp ginger
1 tsp turmeric
2 tsp paprika
2 tsp garam masala
1 lemon
1 tsp salt
300ml natural yogurt
8 panga fillets (haddock or cod could be used)

Method

1 Preheat the oven to 180C / 350F / Gas Mark 4. Finely chop the garlic and ginger.

2 To make the tandoori mixture: add the salt and all the spices together. Squeeze the juice from the lemon and add to the mix with the garlic, ginger and yogurt.

3 Coat the panga fillets evenly with marinade and put into the fridge for 1–1½ hours.

4 Place the fish onto a baking tray and bake for 5–10 minutes or until the flesh is tender. Alternatively, the fillets can be grilled or barbequed.

5 Serve panga fillets with saag aloo potato salad, mint yogurt and salad leaves.

This can be a starter or main course.

courtesy of Keith Perry

Panga Tandoori

poultry

...fed Chicken with Sweet Potato Mash • Chicken Smiley
...hicken Curry with Egg Fried Rice • Dad's Chicken Korm...
...key or Chicken Boobs • Murgh Pilow Served with Dahe...
...ney Mustard Chicken • Chicken Tikka with Savoury Ric...
...Supreme • The World's Hottest Chicken Curry • Crocke...
...with Chicken and Beans • Chicken Satay with Pemmica...
...ht Slims' Cold Chicken • Brie Stuffed Chicken with Swee...
...Mash • Chicken Smiley • Chinese Chicken Curry with Eg...
...Rice • Dad's Chicken Korma • Turkey or Chicken Boobs...
...ow Served with Dahee Chatt • Honey Mustard Chicken...

My Hero
Apollo 11 Crew:
Neil Armstrong, Michael Collins and Buzz Aldrin

At a time in the '60s when the world was preoccupied with the Cold War, US Civil Liberties, the Vietnam War, Sputnik, the Berlin Wall, miniskirts and the Beatles, three men hurtled into space onboard Apollo 11. The crew of Neil Armstrong, Edwin 'Buzz' Aldrin and Michael Collins embarked on a massively brave and courageous journey to the moon whilst the world held its breath. Those eight days in space gave the people on Earth an opportunity to come together in a moment of awe, wonder and unity. This is why these three men are my heroes.

Brie Stuffed Chicken with Sweet Potato Mash
Ingredients

1 chicken breast
85g brie
1 garlic clove
handful of chopped basil, parsley (fresh or dried)
2 tsp oil
1 sweet potato
1 tsp each chopped dill & thyme (fresh or dried)
dash of cream
1 tsp butter
85g string beans

Method

1 Preheat oven to 200C / 425F / Gas Mark 7.

2 Using separate chopping boards, cut a slit down the side of the chicken breast. Cut the brie into small pieces and mix with the herbs, garlic and salt and pepper, next stuff the cheese mixture inside the chicken breast.

3 Heat the oil in a pan and seal the stuffed chicken breast on both sides for a few minutes, seasoning well with salt and pepper. Put the chicken in the oven and cook for a further 15–20 minutes. You must ensure the chicken is cooked through and is not pink on the inside.

4 While the chicken is cooking, cut the sweet potato into small cubes and boil in slightly salted water until tender, drain the water and return potato to the pan.

5 Add the herbs, cream and butter and mash until smooth, season with salt and pepper to taste.

6 Cook the beans in boiling salted water.

7 Serve the chicken breast on a bed of the mash, with the cooked beans on the side.

Brie Stuffed Chicken with Sweet Potato Mash

DIFFICULTY LEVEL	PREPARATION TIME	COOKING TIME	SERVES
EASY	15 MINUTES	20 MINUTES	1

Sergeant Dawn Bailey
RAF Chef

My Hero
Kirsty Howard

My hero is Kirsty Howard, a little girl who has touched the hearts of many. She suffers from a very rare condition where her heart is back to front and abnormal blood vessels have formed in her lung. The condition is so rare that it doesn't even have a name. Kirsty was only expected to live until the end of 1999, but she is still busy raising money for other poorly children. Whenever you see Kirsty on the TV (receiving a Child of Courage award or as one of David Beckham's mascots) she has always got the biggest smile on her face; that's why I named my dish Chicken Smiley.

Chicken Smiley
Ingredients

3 chicken breasts
1 onion
8 button mushrooms
75g butter
25g plain flour
275ml hot milk
½ tsp fennel seeds
200g basmati rice (long grain will work as well)
850ml pints hot chicken stock
2 split cardamom pods
1 crushed garlic clove
½ tsp cumin
½ tsp ground coriander
½ tsp turmeric
½ tsp garam masala
½ tsp ground ginger
oil for frying

Method

1 First, slice the chicken into thin strips next, on a different chopping board, slice the mushrooms and cut the onion into small dice, set this aside until needed.

2 Melt 25g butter in a small pan, keep on a medium heat. When melted, add the flour to make a roux, cook for two minutes, stirring all time, gradually add the hot milk, constantly stirring. Turn the heat down and leave to simmer for 20 minutes, stirring occasionally.

3 Next, melt the 50g butter in another small pan and add the rice and fennel seeds, keep in the heat and stir the rice to coat in the butter completely, stir in the cardamom pods, add the hot stock, cover with cling film, then turn off the heat and leave untouched for 15 minutes.

Chicken Smiley

DIFFICULTY LEVEL	PREPARATION TIME	COOKING TIME	SERVES
EASY	20 MINUTES	30 MINUTES	2

4 Heat the oil in a larger pan and add the chicken, stir for a couple of minutes, add the onion and garlic and cook gently for a couple of minutes, not allowing the onions or chicken to take on any colour, next add the mushrooms, Cook for 3–4 minutes to soften.

5 Now, add the curry spices and cook while stirring to release the flavours.

6 Add the sauce, turn the heat down and simmer for 10 minutes, ensure your chicken is cooked and season with salt and pepper to taste.

7 Serve immediately on the cooked rice.

My Hero

Corporal Lee Daniel Gayler

It was with a great deal of anxiety to the family when our eldest son Lee announced he was going to be attached to the 1 Royal Anglian for a tour of duty in Afghanistan in the summer of 2007. We felt extremely proud while at the same time understandably apprehensive of the obvious dangers that lay ahead.

At 6 a.m. on a bank holiday weekend, we got the 'dreaded call': Lee had been shot during the night whilst on a clearance operation with the fire support group based in Kajaki.

He was airlifted to Camp Bastion where he underwent two operations to remove a bullet that had entered his groin, fracturing his hip socket, just missing his femoral artery by a few millimetres!

On his return to Britain he underwent rehabilitation at Headley Court.

Lee will always be our own hero, but we never forget the many others who continue to risk their lives on a daily basis in the war-stricken areas.

We felt extremely proud while at the same time understandably apprehensive of the obvious dangers that lay ahead.

84

Dad's Chicken Korma

Ingredients

4cm-piece ginger
4 cloves garlic
1 kg skinless chicken breasts
150ml natural yogurt
6 tbsp ghee or vegetable oil
2 onions
½ tsp red chilli powder (optional)
1 tbsp coriander
1 tbsp cumin
good pinch of black pepper
4cm-stick cinnamon
100ml creamed coconut
50g ground almonds
little salt to taste
chopped coriander (optional)

Method

1 Peel the ginger and garlic and place into a blender with three tablespoons of water and blitz to a smooth paste.

2 Dice the chicken and transfer to a bowl, add the yogurt and cover. Chill overnight.

3 Peel and dice the onions, heat ghee or oil in a pan, add the onions and cook until they turn brownish, add the spices and cook gently for 3–4 minutes.

4 Add the chicken and marinade. Raise the heat, add 300ml of water and bring to the boil.

5 Add coconut and almonds and cook gently on a simmer for about 30–40 minutes, turning the chicken over now and then.

6 Season to taste, sprinkle with chopped coriander to serve.

7 Serve with basmati rice, delicious!!!

DIFFICULTY LEVEL	PREPARATION TIME	COOKING TIME	SERVES
MODERATE	20 MINUTES (NEEDS TO MARINADE OVERNIGHT)	45 MINUTES	4

Dame Vera Lynn
Singer, Entertainer and The Forces' Sweetheart

My Hero
Our Brave Serving Men and Women

Having met so many wonderful servicemen and women during the Second World War years and after, it is always very interesting and satisfying to know that in some small way I was able to make them feel as if home was not too far away when they were serving abroad, especially in far flung places like Burma. People don't seem to learn from history as the wars since the Second World War and the current conflicts testify. The boys and girls attitudes and courage to fight for their country has in no way diminished. I understand that I am mentioned in Afghanistan and Iraq by the brave serving men and women, which is a great surprise and pleasure to me. I wish them all the very best and to let them know that we are all thinking about them, whether in the air, on the ground or on the sea.

Turkey or Chicken Boobs
Ingredients
2 turkey or chicken breasts
2 medium onions
2 cloves garlic
3 tomatoes
250g button mushrooms
250ml stock

Method

1 Peel and chop the onions. Saute the onions then add the breasts.

2 Peel and finely chop the garlic and add to the mixture.

3 Skin and finely chop the tomatoes and add to the mixture.

4 Finely slice the mushrooms and add to the mixture.

5 Add stock, season, cover and simmer until tender (turkey will take longer than chicken).

This is a simple and healthy but very tasty dish.

DIFFICULTY LEVEL	PREPARATION TIME	COOKING TIME	SERVES
EASY	20 MINUTES	25 MINUTES	2

Turkey or Chicken Boobs

My Hero
Jonah Lomu

My hero is undoubtedly the dynamic and powerful All Blacks rugby player, Jonah Lomu, the first true global superstar of Rugby Union. Being a keen rugby player myself I would often watch in amazement at the power of Jonah on the field. I will never forget watching him quite literally run through Mike Catt in the 1995 World Cup Semi-Final against England; the devastation felt as he seemed to be single-handedly knocking England out of the competition alongside an overwhelming feeling of awe and admiration, acknowledging that with this man mountain, a new chapter in rugby history had arrived.

At the end of 1996, at just twenty-eight years old, he commenced a ten-year battle with a rare kidney disorder forcing an early departure from rugby at all levels. Extraordinarily, this was not the anticipated end of his career that many medical experts predicted, and in 2004 he made an explosive comeback after undergoing a kidney transplant to again play rugby at the highest levels.

In that same year I became seriously injured and was confined to a wheelchair for six months. I was unable to walk and was told that I would never play rugby again. Watching Jonah Lomu that year defy all laws of medicine made me determined that I would recover and would prove the doctors wrong.

I returned to RN rugby this season and played against the Army and the RAF at the Inter-Services! I believe that the inspiration from watching Jonah's extraordinary journey helped me to achieve my goal of playing rugby once again for the Royal Navy.

This recipe has everything a rugby player could ask for: carbs, veg and masses of protein. If Jonah were to come for dinner this is what I would make for him.

Jonah Lomu courtesy of The Sun/NI Syndication

Murgh Pilow served with Dahee Chaat

DIFFICULTY LEVEL	PREPARATION TIME	COOKING TIME	SERVES
MODERATE	45 MINUTES	20 MINUTES	4

Ingredients

Pilow:
1 whole chicken
475g rice
1 bulb garlic
1 small piece ginger
3 medium onions
1250ml water
1 whole garam masala (optional)
1 tbsp salt
2 bay leaves
1 chicken stock cube (optional)
3 heaped tbsp frozen peas

Chaat:
2 large potatoes
2 medium onions
10 green chillies (vary according to taste, but should be quite hot)
1 can chickpeas
salt to taste
1 large pot yogurt

Method

1 Cut chicken into 8 pieces, bones left in. Wash rice thoroughly, leave to soak in water. Peel and finely chop garlic and ginger and, separately, the onions.

2 Put half the garlic and ginger, one of the onions, the garam masala and water in a large pan with the chicken pieces. Bring to the boil and simmer the stock for thirty minutes. Season and add bay leaves, and a stock cube if you wish.

3 Brown remaining onions in the oil until almost charred, making the dish a lovely golden colour. Add a small ladle of stock, cover immediately with tight-fitting lid until the hissing stops!!

4 Add the remaining ginger and garlic; cook until the stock has significantly reduced. Add salt and garam masala, fry for a few more minutes.

5 Remove onions and masala from stock, add to the fry mixture. Don't add more stock yet. Fry for another minute, then add the chicken pieces, brown them for 5 minutes, then add peas and cook for 2 minutes.

6 Sieve the stock and add the liquid to the pan. Bring it to the boil, then add the drained rice. Keep boiling, stirring occasionally, until the liquid is nearly all gone, but the rice still appears wet.

7 Reduce heat to its lowest setting, put on a tight-fitting lid, or cover with cling film, ensuring no steam escapes.

8 For the chaat: boil the peeled and cubed potatoes in salted water, until soft but not mushy. Drain and cool.

9 Chop the onions and chillies, add the drained, rinsed chick peas, salt, potatoes and yogurt, mix into a thick creamy sauce. Add a little milk, if it appears too thick.

To serve, fluff the rice with a fork, being careful not to break the rice. Serve the chaat separately

Lieutenant Colonel John Stroud-Turp
Royal Artillery Officer

My Hero
Private Harry Schofield – My Grandfather

My grandfather was born in 1890 in a small Yorkshire mining village, one of thirteen children of whom four died in infancy; by the age of thirteen he was 'working down't pits', as they say in Yorkshire, hauling the coal his father dug. In 1916 he exchanged the dangers of mining for those of the Western Front, where he served almost continuously until the end of the war. Twice, possibly three times, he survived major offensives that left the vast majority of his battalion dead or wounded – this led to him serving with three different regiments, as surviving soldiers were reallocated to reconstitute depleted regiments. I still have a collection of his cap badges and collar/shoulder badges. After the war he returned to the mines and the uncertain future of the 1920s and '30s where he became actively involved in the miners' union, despite the deep unpopularity of unionization amongst the mine owners. He finally retired in 1957 aged sixty-seven, ten years after the nationalization of the mines.

Grandfather died in 1980 aged almost ninety-one. I was a teenager when he died and never fully appreciated the wealth and depth of his experiences; I remember

my grandfather as a quiet, dignified man with an incredibly positive outlook on life bolstered by a great mental and physical robustness – perhaps surviving the Western Front and over fifty years of mining instils this in a man. Like many of his generation he rarely discussed his war-time experiences – maybe now, with over twenty-five years of professional soldiering behind me, we could have a conversation about his own rather intense experiences of soldiering – I hesitate to say 'swap war stories' as I believe my own experiences would pale into insignificance when compared to his. I would also be fascinated to hear about his life in the mines and I try to understand the rich seam of social and industrial history that ran through his life, especially the poverty and hardships of the post-Great War years.

The relative poverty of his upbringing meant Grandfather would eat and enjoy almost anything – pig's brain and butter or tripe with onions springs to mind. However, I believe he would really enjoy lemon and honey chicken, and perhaps afterwards we could sit by the fire with a glass of his favourite malt and talk about life and the universe.

Honey and Mustard Chicken

Ingredients

4 skinless chicken breasts (preferably free range)
2 lemons
3 cloves garlic
3 tbsp honey
2 tbsp olive oil
3 tbsp whole grain mustard
¼ tsp paprika (optional)
80g butter
salt
black pepper
basmati rice for 4 people.

Method

1 Preheat the oven to 190C / 375F / Gas Mark 5

2 Cut the chicken into strips approximately 6–8cm long and about 2 cm wide.

3 Squeeze the juice from the two lemons.

4 Arrange the chicken strips onto a baking tray.

5 Peel and finely chop the garlic.

6 Soften the butter over a low heat, remove from the heat and add the honey, garlic olive oil, paprika and mustard, season well with salt and pepper.

7 Spoon the mixture over the chicken, then pour over the lemon juice. Ensure all the pieces are covered with sauce.

8 Place near the top of the oven for 20 minutes.

9 Cook the rice of your choice as specified on the box (or choose one of the rice recipes from elsewhere in this book).

10 Grill the chicken and sauces under a medium grill, for about 4 minutes or until the chicken begins to brown. You need to watch to ensure the chicken does not burn.

DIFFICULTY LEVEL	PREPARATION TIME	COOKING TIME	SERVES
EASY	10 MINUTES	25 MINUTES	4

11 Serve the chicken on a bed of rice with the sauce spooned over the chicken.

Corporal Steve Atkin
Army Junior Non-Commissioned Officer and Firefighter

My Hero
Stephanie Atkin
(wife, friend and soulmate)

I would cook this hero's meal for my wife Stephanie, as I know she loves a good Indian takeaway. Stephanie has been in my life forever: we went to the same primary school and then secondary school and started going out together when we were there.

From early in our marriage, Stephanie has always supported me and given me self-belief, and she gave me confidence when I first left the Army and started out in 'civvy street'. Eventually Stephanie and I had three lovely children, Lauren, Hannah and Megan. In 2004 I joined the Fire Service and was called up as a Reservist to serve in Afghanistan in 2007. Again Stephanie was a rock not only to our children but also to my mum and dad, and she kept all of our spirits up.

In December 2007 I was injured on the front line whilst liberating the town of Musa Qaleh and was flown back to England where I have been getting treatment since. I have at times found myself feeling very low because of my injuries and will always be grateful to my Stephanie for her support and endless love.

Chicken Tikka with Savoury Rice
Ingredients
Tikka paste:
1 tsp cumin
1 tsp dry coriander
1 tsp chilli powder
1 tsp ground cardamom
1 tsp cayenne pepper
1 tsp paprika
2 tsp garam masala
1 lemon
300ml natural yogurt
1 whole chicken

Savoury rice:
2 onions
2 chillies
200g rice
750ml water or stock

Chicken Tikka with Savoury Rice

Method

1 Preheat the oven to 170C / 325F / Gas Mark 3.

2 To make the paste, mix all the spices together and add the yogurt. Squeeze the juice from the lemon and add to the mixture.

3 Next, skin and portion the chicken into eight, by cutting each breast and each leg into half.

4 Coat all the chicken pieces in the marinade (this is best left overnight).

5 Place the chicken onto a baking tray and cook for 25 minutes. Time will vary, depending on the size of the chicken.

6 For the rice, finely chop the onions and chillies, then cook in a non-stick pan until soft. Add the rice and cook for a further one minute. Add the water or stock, bring to the boil and simmer on a medium heat for 10 minutes, stirring occasionally so the rice does not stick.

7 Serve with naan bread and onion bhaji with mint yogurt and garnish with coriander.

This can be served as a starter or main course.

DIFFICULTY LEVEL	PREPARATION TIME	COOKING TIME	SERVES
MODERATE	30-40 MINUTES	25 MINUTES	4

93

My Hero
Bruce Lee

He was only 5'6" with terrible eyesight, but his pure passion for martial arts allowed him to overcome racism and physical inabilities. Bruce Lee was instrumental in completely changing the western world's views on oriental culture and martial arts. I don't believe there is a finer example of what can be achieved through dedication and self-motivation, and that's what always keeps me going when I'm physically exhausted.

Chicken Supreme
Ingredients

2 small onions
3 cloves garlic
4 rashers bacon
4 skinless chicken breasts
1 chicken stock cube
100ml boiling water
400ml cream
50g sweet corn
450g rice
1200ml boiling water
salt and pepper
oil for cooking

Method

1 Dice the onions and finely chop the garlic.

2 Fry the onion and garlic until golden, then remove from the pan.

3 Dice the bacon and fry off, and then remove from the pan.

4 Fry the chicken until cooked and add the onion, garlic and bacon.

5 Add the stock cube to the 100ml of boiling water and add to the chicken. Then add the cream, the sweet corn and season. Cook for a further 10 minutes.

6 For the rice, add the rice to the 1200ml of boiling water. Boil for 15 minutes, turn off the heat and cover with cling film for 15 minutes, then serve with the chicken.

Chicken Supreme

Andy McNab
Ex-Special Forces and Author

My Hero
Ernest Shackleton

Ernest Shackleton is my ultimate hero. He was a fine explorer, but it is his courage, leadership and determination in times of adversity that impress me most of all. Shackleton's famous expedition across the Antarctic reads like a thriller. When his boat Endurance is crushed by ice, he and his men are forced to survive on an ice floe for two months, in the hope that it will drift towards safety.

But when the ice floe breaks in two, Shackleton has to take immediate action. He gets his men into three lifeboats, and they head for Elephant Island from where he hopes they will be rescued.

On arrival, he discovers the island is an inhospitable place, and there is no chance of them being discovered. Shackleton changes tack. He and five of his crew sail in one of the lifeboats a further eight hundred miles across stormy, ice-filled seas to South Georgia in the hope that they will be rescued by whalers there. They find it very difficult to find a place to land their boat safely. Eventually, they manage to get into a bay on the south of the island. But they still aren't saved because they are on the uninhabited side of the island. To get

to the whaling stations for help, someone would have to cross the unmapped island to the other side. This would mean climbing high mountains that had never been crossed before.

But Shackleton doesn't give up. He takes two of the team with him and, covering forty miles in thirty-six hours, reaches a whaling station on the other side of the island. Without delay he then sends out a party to pick up the crew on the south side of the island, while he returns to Elephant Island to pick up his remaining men. Not a single man in either of the two parties loses his life.

My bookshelves are lined with books about his epic journey. I have even gone to the Antarctic myself to see the landscape and to get a feel for what he might have experienced out there. His leadership skills and sheer physical and mental stamina are truly inspirational. I would love to cook him dinner. I reckon I would cook him the world's hottest chicken curry, and I think he would have been gagging for it.

The World's Hottest Chicken Curry

Method

1 Cut the chicken into bite-size pieces, and then set aside. Next, make a paste from the curry and chilli powders, with the addition of a little water, and set this aside too.

2 Dice the onion and place to one side. Then cut the chillis, garlic and ginger into a fine dice, even using a blender if you wish.

3 Heat the oil in a large saute pan, add the onion and fry gently for two minutes to soften.

4 Stir in the chilli, garlic and ginger mix and fry for a further few minutes. Add the curry or chilli paste you have made and fry for 30 seconds more, stirring constantly to release the flavours.

5 Add the chicken pieces and seal the meat on all sides, stir in half the gravy and simmer gently for 20 minutes or until the chicken is cooked, stirring regularly. If needed, add more gravy or water to prevent the curry becoming too thick or dry.

6 Next, add the garam masala and chopped coriander and cook for a further minute.

7 Taste and see if it needs any salt, serve on a bed of rice with the whole coriander leaves sprinkled on top.

Ingredients

4 chicken breasts
5 tsp curry powder
2 tsp chilli powder
1 onion
2 Cayenne chillies (or any chilli)
6 cloves garlic
5cm-piece root ginger
5 tbsp vegetable oil
1 cup curry masala gravy (curry gravy)
4 tbsp coriander leaves
2 tsp garam masala
1 tbsp whole coriander leaves

DIFFICULTY LEVEL	PREPARATION TIME	COOKING TIME	SERVES
EASY	15 MINUTES	30 MINUTES	2

This serves 2, but I think Shackleton deserves a double portion!

My Hero
Muhammad Ali

Being an avid sports fan and having played competitive sports for as long as I can remember, I would have to regard Muhammad Ali as my hero. He was the first person to become three times heavyweight world champion, winning fifty-seven of his sixty-one pro fights, thirty-seven of them by knockout. His will to win was shown from an early age when he won the Olympic light heavyweight gold medal six years after he started boxing. He not only overcame fifty-seven of his opponents, but also the political system and racism throughout his career. He was awarded sports personality of the century by the BBC in 1999. He continues to fight and raise money to this day, no longer in the ring but against Parkinson's disease. Probably the most recognised person on the planet and a massive inspiration to a lot of people: this is why he is my hero.

Richard is a Junior Non-Commissioned Officer who was awarded the Military Cross for showing exceptional courage when aiding the crew of a stricken Mastiff armoured vehicle under repeated Taliban attacks. He braved enemy rocket and small-arms fire to recover the vehicle and force it through an enemy ambush. His citation comments on how he 'maintained tempo at a critical time and undoubtedly prevented significant casualties from being taken. He was a credit to his Squadron and Corps and his was a conspicuous display of gallantry.'

Crocked Tortillas with Chicken and Beans

Ingredients

1 lemon
1 onion
a few sprigs parsley
2 chicken breasts
½ tsp onion powder
½ tsp celery seed
salt and pepper
4 tbsp water
½ tbsp oil
1 garlic clove
200ml enchilada sauce
200ml tomato sauce
1x450g can baked beans or pinto beans
100g sweetcorn
4 tortillas
250g grated cheese
6 black olives

Crocked Tortillas with Chicken and Beans

DIFFICULTY LEVEL	PREPARATION TIME	COOKING TIME	SERVES
EASY	15 MINUTES	40 MINUTES	4

Method

1 First, pre-heat the oven to 180C / 350F / Gas Mark 4. Slice the lemon and half of the onion.

2 Add the chicken breast into an oven-proof dish, then add the sliced onions, lemon, onion powder, celery seed, parsley, salt, pepper and water.

3 Cover and cook in the oven for 25 minutes.

4 Shred the chicken when cooked.

5 Slice the other half of the onion, crush the garlic and lightly fry in a little oil. Add the chicken and continue frying until brown.

6 Stir together the chilli sauce, beans and corn.

7 Grease a suitably sized oven-proof dish.

8 Lay the first tortilla and spread ⅓ of the chicken, ⅓ of the bean mix, ¼ of the cheese.

9 Repeat this two more times.

10 Add the last tortilla, sprinkle on the last ¼ of the cheese.

11 Add the olives and lay on top of the cheese.

12 Cook in the oven for a further 30 minutes.

My Hero
Captain Robert Falcon Scott

Captain Scott was an inspirational explorer who pioneered from the front to embark on one of the world's greatest challenges: to travel unsupported to the geographic South Pole. The death of him and his team only eleven miles from 1 Tonne Depot and from survival has posed many questions into his character, but unless you've experienced Antarctica herself, you really can't appreciate the outstanding courage that he demonstrated to lead his team so far. Captain Scott was my inspiration to lead the first-ever unsupported military attempt to the South Pole in 2006. My team were only five days away from achieving our goal, when a team member became so ill that we were unable to finish the six hundred miles. Unlike Captain Scott's team we all came back alive, but without his zest and enthusiasm for adventure I never would have thought of attempting such a feat.

Chicken Satay with Pemmican

Ingredients

1 x 250ml carton pineapple juice
5 heaped tbsp peanut butter
1 tsp dried sage
3 tsp chilli bean sauce
5 large spring onions
Salt and pepper
6 chicken breasts
12 wooden skewers
(soaked in water for at least an hour)
4 large bell peppers (multi colors)
1 packet pemmican
150g basmati rice per person

Method

1 The day before your meal make the marinade: put all the marinade ingredients (pineapple juice, peanut butter, sage, chilli sauce and finely-chopped spring onions) in a bowl and mix. Season well with the salt and pepper.

2 Cut the chicken into chunks, put them onto the sticks, lay them on a plate and spoon over the marinade, cover and leave in the fridge overnight.

3 The next morning, chop the mixed coloured peppers into 2–inch square chunks, soak the basmati rice and add the pemmican.

4 Slowly grill the chicken sticks, reserving and boiling up any leftover sauce; thickening with cornflour if needed.

5 Boil your rice, this will only take 10 minutes as it has been soaked, remember to wash the starch off the rice with boiling water once cooked.

Chicken Satay with Pemmican

DIFFICULTY LEVEL	PREPARATION TIME	COOKING TIME	SERVES
EASY	20 MINUTES	15 MINUTES PLUS MARINADE OVERNIGHT	6

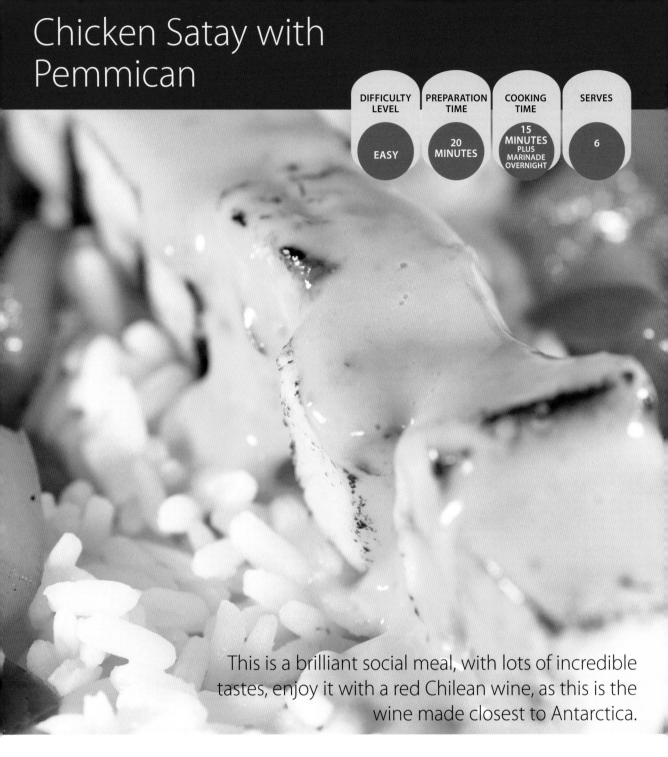

This is a brilliant social meal, with lots of incredible tastes, enjoy it with a red Chilean wine, as this is the wine made closest to Antarctica.

6 Flash fry the peppers and serve them crunchy.

7 Lay the rice as a bed, slice bits of pemmican and put on the rice. Lay out the multicolored peppers around the edge of the plate and lay your chicken sticks over the center, pouring the excess sauce over.

Pemmican is a nutritious mixture of fat and protein invented by the Native Indians of North American. It is often used as an emergency high-energy foodstuff, particularly good for extreme environments.

My Hero

Field Marshal The Viscount Slim

General Sir William Slim (D 25026) by permission of the Imperial War Museum

Field Marshal The Viscount Slim is my abiding hero because in a world war of many well-known characters he was the Commander who demonstrated the highest levels of generalship in the most difficult circumstances. He transformed the 'Forgotten Army' in Burma, through his own personality and skill, into a fighting force that genuinely turned defeat into victory and had a major impact on the conduct and subsequent success of the Allies in the Far East. His example of leadership, organisational skills and the ability to outmanoeuvre an enemy in time and space stands as an inspiration to all. Knowing that he led an Army with British, Commonwealth, Gurkha and Indian soldiers, I have chosen a menu that I think would have appealed to all those under his command – a cold curried chicken dish. It can be made hotter for those who like spicy foods, or cool for those like me who prefer interesting food on a more temperate plane! It is also a great favourite with the Dannatt family and easy to make.

Viscount Slim's Cold Chicken in a Curried Mayonnaise

Infinitely superior to simple Coronation Chicken!

Ingredients

2 small cooked chickens
325ml double cream
3 tbsp white or red wine vinegar
2 tbsp runny honey
1 heaped tbsp medium curry powder
8 tbsp mayonnaise
chopped parsley to garnish

Method

1 Take all the meat off the chickens, being careful to exclude all little bones and gristle. Chop the meat into bite size pieces.

2 To make the sauce, whisk the cream until it reaches the soft-peak stage. Mix in the vinegar, honey and curry powder (adding more if you like it spicy) into the mayonnaise, then fold the mayonnaise into the cream.

3 Just before serving, stir the sauce into the chicken and serve with new potatoes and a green salad or cous cous, as an alternative. Delicious.

If I were to follow this up with a dessert, it would have to be strawberries and cream. As simple a dessert as any, but very hard to beat and quintessentially British. It would remind any hero of home!

Viscount Slim's Cold Chicken in a Curried Mayonnaise

DIFFICULTY LEVEL	PREPARATION TIME	COOKING TIME	SERVES
VERY EASY	15 MINUTES	0 MINUTES	8

My Hero
Sir Alan Cobham

Sir Alan was an RFC pilot in the First World War, and devoted much of his time as a test pilot for de Havilland. He carried out many overseas flights, his flying taking him to many European cities and to such places as Singapore and Australia. He was responsible for getting the public air-minded, using a combination of barnstorming and joy-riding. He gathered a number of aircraft, single seaters and passenger airliners, together with their pilots. They toured the country with what became known as 'Cobham's Flying Circus'. It was extremely popular, giving the public their first opportunity to fly, to meet the pilots and to take an interest in aviation.

It was on one visit from the Circus that I was taken on a flight from Renfrew airfield. I remember it well: a large biplane, flown by none other than Sir Alan himself, awe-inspiring to a lad of twelve years. It cost my dad all of five shillings. What a story I could tell my school classmates. It did not stop there; I nearly always got the opportunity when the Circus was in town to repeat the thrill of flying with other pilots such as Capt O. P. Jones, and Capt. W. E. Johns (both of Imperial Airways), the latter the author of the Biggles books.

All these contacts coupled with Sir Alan's superb illustrated lectures on his experiences were a great inspiration to me as a boy, and I decided that I would fly myself. To achieve this I had to join the RAF. I had a goal.

Nothing seemed to daunt Sir Alan, he was a great pioneer of aviation in general; he devoted much of his time to air-to-air refuelling, demonstrating the system at the Circus venue in the early 1930s. A far-seeing visionary, the air-to-air refuelling company that bears his name stills exist today. Where would the Air Forces of today be without his idea?

Truly a man of many talents, foresight, spirit of adventure and tenacity, Sir Alan inspired me.

My choice of a meal for this true pioneer aviator would be good Chinese chicken curry.

Chinese Chicken Curry with Egg Fried Rice and Prawn Crackers

Ingredients

4 chicken breasts
1 large onion
100g butter or margarine
90g flour
20g curry powder
1 litre hot chicken stock
200g rice
2 litres vegetable stock
3 tbsp oil
100g peas
2 beaten eggs
2 tbsp soy sauce
prawn crackers to serve

Method

1 First prepare your ingredients: remove all the fat from the chicken and cut into strips. Set aside and, on a different chopping board, peel and slice your onion.

2 Next make the sauce: melt the butter or margarine in a sauce pan, stir in the flour and curry powder and cook over a low heat, stirring constantly for a few minutes to cook the flour. Add the hot chicken stock a little at a time, being very careful not to burn yourself, stirring the liquid in, until you achieve a sauce consistency that coats the back of a spoon, adding more or less stock as needed.

3 Leave the sauce over a very low heat to cook for 20 minutes, stirring often to prevent the sauce burning. The sauce may thicken when cooking out, so more stock might need to be added.

4 Next put the rice in a saucepan and cover with the stock, bring it to the boil. Simmer for 5 minutes, then turn the heat off and tightly cover the pan with cling film. Leave for 20 minutes for the stock to be absorbed by the rice.

5 Now to make the curry: heat 2 tablespoons of the oil in a pan and fry the onions for 5 minutes, until starting to turn brown but still a bit crunchy. Remove from the pan with a slotted spoon and set aside.

6 Next cook the chicken in the pan until cooked through. Add the peas and pour over the sauce, stir thoroughly and keep warm.

7 For the rice: heat the remaining oil in a wok and fry the egg until cooked. Add the rice and fry for 2 minutes, stir in the soy sauce and set aside.

8 Just before serving the curry, stir the onions back into the sauce. Serve immediately with a generous helping of curry and rice with prawn crackers on the side to scoop up all the goodness!

DIFFICULTY LEVEL	PREPARATION TIME	COOKING TIME	SERVES
EASY	10 MINUTES	45 MINUTES	4

SQUADRON LEADER
JOHN BLAIR DFM

Squadron Leader (Retired) John Blair DFM (known as Ian) joined the RAF in 1934 at the age of 16 as one of the first boy entrant apprentices (Service No. 550006), and is now the senior living boy apprentice.

After some years working as an armourer, he retrained as a gunner on Blenheims. During a subsequent operational sortie, he earned the Distinguished Flying Medal for bringing an aircraft back safely after the pilot had been killed. He was then selected for pilot training in 1941 as part of the Empire Training scheme, in Nairobi, then Habbanyia, Iraq, and finally Rhodesia. He was successful and was posted back to the UK in 1942 to No 501 Squadron, Ibsley, as a sergeant Spitfire pilot. He flew some 20 operational hours, before being hospitalised following a forced landing as a result of enemy action.

Subsequently he was posted to No 602 'City of Glasgow' Squadron as a Flight Sergeant Spitfire pilot from where, after completing an 18 month tour and about 140 sorties, he was posted away from

operational duties (now as a Flight Lieutenant and with a new Service No. 53630) to a specialist armament course for general duties officers.

You may have seen a classic security poster of the time: 'Careless Talk May Cost His Life' – well that was Acting Sergeant Ian Blair DFM (a copy is shown below – and one of the originals is on show in the RAF Museum).

Ian eventually retired as a Squadron Leader supply officer in 1973 but he has continued to retain his links with the RAF, by very active involvement as Secretary of the local branch of the RAF Aircrew Association, in Essex. He is also involved with the Spitfire Association and the Blenheim Association, and he also works as a guide at the RAF Museum, Hendon.

pork

...mbled Pork with Pasta and Tomato Sauce • Pease Pud...
...ork Fillet with Pesto • Sweet and Sour Pork • Herb-crur...
...with Pasta and Tomato Sauce • Pease Pudding • Stuffe...
...with Pesto • Sweet and Sour Pork • Herb-crumbled Por...
...and Tomato Sauce • Pease Pudding • Stuffed Pork Fille...
... • Sweet and Sour Pork • Herb-crumbled Pork with Past...
...atoe Sauce • Pease Pudding • Stuffed Pork Fillet with F...
...and Sour Pork • Herb-crumbled Pork with Pasta and To...
... • Pease Pudding • Stuffed Pork Fillet with Pesto • Swe...
... • Herb-crumbled Pork with Pasta and Tomato Sauce...

My Hero

Royal Australian Signals Corporal Colin 'Doc' Judd

28 Commonwealth Brigade, Malaya, 1962, was my first posting and many of us 'raw' nineteen-year-olds were struggling in the oppressive heat and mosquito- and leech-infested jungles. Doc was an experienced Aussie corporal who readily passed on his survival tips and made life more bearable for all of us; he was highly respected by everyone. Doc was subsequently selected to join the highly decorated Australian Army Training Team Vietnam, whose members operated in small groups throughout southern Vietnam. Doc spent his time in the Central Highlands training and fighting with the montagnards (ethnic mountain people) and, when I went to live in Vietnam some forty years later, he immediately asked me to try to visit the montagnards, whom he believed were being treated unfairly for having helped the Americans and Australians in the Vietnam War. Many soldiers display courage, as Doc always did, but few are also able to consistently display such compassion for their fellow man. He's a hero in my eyes.

Herb-crumbed Pork with Pasta and Tomato Sauce

Ingredients

10 tomatoes
1 onion
3 cloves garlic
8 basil leaves
8 sprigs tarragon
200ml red wine
2 tbsp white wine vinegar
2 tbsp caster sugar
2 tbsp tomato puree
600ml chicken stock
salt and pepper
2 pork steaks
75g flour
1 egg
4 slices of bread
herbs of your choice
2 tbsp olive oil
large knob butter
200g pasta

Herb-crumbed Pork with Pasta and Tomato Sauce

Method

1 For the sauce, dice the tomatoes and onion.

2 Crush the garlic and finely chop the herbs.

3 Fry off the garlic and onions in a little oil until soft. Add the red wine, white wine vinegar and caster sugar.

4 Now add the tomato paste, tomatoes and stock. Cook for about an hour on low heat.

5 Add basil, tarragon and season.

6 While the sauce is cooking out, take all the fat off the pork steak and batten out slightly.

7 Crumb down the bread (this can be done in a food processor).

8 Mix some herbs to the crumb mix.

9 Now get 3 small bowls, put flour and season into one, beaten egg into another and bread crumbs into another.

10 Now coat the pork through the flour, eggs and bread crumbs.

11 Shallow fry in some oil and butter and finish in the oven for approximately 10 minutes.

12 While the pork is in the oven, add the pasta to boiling water and simmer until the pasta is cooked about 10 minutes.

13 To serve, mix the pasta with some of the sauce top with the pork and finish with the sauce.

DIFFICULTY LEVEL	PREPARATION TIME	COOKING TIME	SERVES
EASY	20 MINUTES	10-15 MINUTES	2

Commander I T Roberts OBE
Royal Naval Officer; Former Commanding Officer of HMS Vigilant and HMS Triumph

My Hero
Dr Martin Luther King Jr.

To learn that racial segregation was happening in the USA during my lifetime came as a huge surprise, and the struggle against it under the leadership of Dr King had a profound impact on me as a young man. The success of his peaceful and powerful struggle for civil rights was emphatic with the recent election of the first black President of the USA. The recipe for Pease Pudding is as simple as was the message of Dr King: respect for every human being.

Pease Pudding
Ingredients
1 large ham shank
salt and pepper
470g split peas
125g butter

Method

1 Place the ham shank into a pan of water and bring to the boil.

2 Drain the water and replace with new water and bring to the boil.

3 Place the split peas into muslin cloth and tie. Place this into the pan of water containing the ham shank. Allow it all to simmer for 2 hours.

4 Take out the ham shank and allow the split peas to continue cooking for a further 2 hours.

5 After this time, the split peas should be soft. Empty them from the muslin and mash until they have a nice soft consistency, then add the butter, salt and pepper to taste.

6 If the puree is still too thick, add a little water from the pan until you reach the right consistency.

7 Lovely on a ham sandwich, even better on a baguette.

DIFFICULTY LEVEL	PREPARATION TIME	COOKING TIME	SERVES
EASY	2 MINUTES	4 HOURS	8

Pease Pudding

Jim Broadbent
Actor

My Hero
Leo Tolstoy

My hero is the Russian author, essayist and philosopher Leo Tolstoy, who wrote, among others, the epic novel War and Peace (1865-69), set during the Napoleonic wars and forming the backdrop of his painstakingly detailed depiction of early nineteenth century Tsarist Russia. With masterful development of characters Pierre, Natasha, Andrew, Nicholas, Mary and the rest, War and Peace examines the absurdity, hypocrisy and shallowness of war and aristocratic society.

Almost one hundred years after his death, in January of 2007, Tolstoy's Anna Karenina (1878) and War and Peace were placed on Time magazine's list of the ten greatest novels of all time, first and third place respectively. This longevity of such a thought-provoking masterpiece proves Tolstoy's outstanding writing skill.

Sweet and Sour Pork

Ingredients

Sauce:
3 cloves garlic
100g ginger
100g onions
1 chilli
100g sliced pepper
200ml water
125ml sugar
125ml vinegar
100g tomato puree

Pork and batter:
800g pork (pork loin is good, fillet is better)
10g flour
1 tsp Chinese five spice
100g flour
100ml vinegar
1 tbsp baking powder
200ml water

Method

1 Slice the onions and peppers and finely chop the ginger, garlic and chilli.

2 For the sauce: on the hob heat a little oil in a pan and sweat off the onions, garlic, ginger and chilli.

3 Add water, vinegar, tomato puree and sugar.

4 Bring to the boil and simmer for 15 minutes. Then add the peppers.

5 Simmer for a further 10 minutes and season.

6 Meanwhile, dice the pork to bite-sized pieces.

7 Mix 10g of flour and Chinese spice together and toss the pork in this mix.

Sweet and Sour Pork

DIFFICULTY LEVEL	PREPARATION TIME	COOKING TIME	SERVES
MODERATE	30 MINUTES	10-15 MINUTES	4

8 For the batter, put the water and vinegar into a bowl, add the flour and whisk until you get a smooth texture, add baking powder and whisk again.

9 Now to finish the pork, dip the floured pork into the batter and deep-fry on a moderate heat till golden brown; approx 10–15 minutes. If golden brown but not cooked through, finish in oven pre-heated to 180C / 350F / Gas Mark 4 until cooked through.

10 Add pork to the sauce and serve immediately with either rice or noodles.

Andy Allen
1st Battalion, The Royal Irish Regiment

My Hero
Ranger Grant Fox and Lance Corporal Andrew Kenny

Ranger Grant Fox and Lance Corporal Andrew Kenny are two lads from my Battalion who saved my life. Ranger Fox was the Battalion Photographer and Lance Corporal Kenny was the Team Medic and they just happened to be on that patrol. The actions of Grant and Andy speak far louder than any words I can write can portray. It is entirely due to their quick thinking and actions directly after the IED incident that I am still here.

Stuffed Pork Fillet with Pesto
served with New Potatoes in Rosemary Butter and Seasonal Vegetables

Ingredients

1 pork fillet
½ pear, peeled and sliced into wedges

Chutney:
olive oil
2 cloves garlic, crushed
1 beef tomato chopped
1 small onion, chopped
few sprigs thyme
2 tsp sugar
splash of balsamic vinegar
2 tbsp grated Parmesan

Potatoes:
handful of scrubbed new potatoes
knob of butter
sprig rosemary, chopped
salt and freshly ground black pepper

Pesto:
handful of basil
150ml olive oil
2–3 cloves garlic
salt and freshly ground black pepper

Method

1 Preheat the oven to 200C / 400F / Gas Mark 6

2 To make the pesto, place all the pesto ingredients into a food processor and blend to a smooth puree

3 For the potatoes, boil in slightly salted water until cooked, drain, drop in a knob of butter and chopped rosemary, cover with a lid and lightly toss.

4 To make the chutney, heat the garlic and chopped onion in olive oil for one minute.

Stuffed Pork Fillet with Pesto served with
New Potatoes in Rosemary Butter and Seasonal Vegetables

5 Add the chopped tomato, thyme, sugar and balsamic vinegar. Reduce the vinegar by half.

6 Stir in the grated Parmesan and take the pan off the heat. Leave to cool.

7 Place the pork fillet between two sheets of cling film and beat out using a meat mallet or rolling pin.

8 Put a tablespoon of chutney and a few slices of pear on the pork and roll it up, securing the stuffing with a cocktail stick.

9 Pan-fry the stuffed pork fillet for 3-4 minutes until browned. Place into the oven for 2–3 minutes to cook through.

10 Slice the pork into 2cm-thick slices and lay them next to the new potatoes with a drizzle of basil pesto and serve with seasonal vegetables.

DIFFICULTY LEVEL	PREPARATION TIME	COOKING TIME	SERVES
MODERATE	35 MINUTES	15-30 MINUTES	1

RANGER
ANDY ALLEN

For the first few hours of 14th July 2008 life was normal for Ranger Andy Allen. He took his share of sentry duty at the isolated patrol base which was home for him and the rest of his team. He slept, woke, ate and checked kit in preparation for another patrol into the vegetation of the green zone. He shared a joke with his fellow Royal Irish soldiers, and probably some of the Afghan National Army soldiers with whom he was working. To him, this had become his routine, no different from readying oneself to catch an early morning train to the office. But just after seven in the morning, only a couple of kilometres away from that tranquil scene, Andy Allen lost both legs and, temporarily, his sight.

Kept alive by the most astonishing medical efforts, he has since been on a journey of epic proportions; from the point when he was wounded in a muddy ambush, through his evacuation within Afghanistan, and his flight back to the UK.

As a 19-year-old Ranger he blended in with his crowd. As a 20-year-old veteran of his own campaign to walk and see again, he stands out. Many of us would, I suspect, have slipped away and allowed our world to end in that muddy ambush. Andy Allen did not, does not. Courage and determination are his hallmarks, and those who have served in his company look upon him as a true hero.

His world did not end at that moment;
it was just irrevocably changed.

lamb

houlder of Lamb • North African Lamb with Ginger an
• Mint Lamb Chops with Roasted Shallots and Spinac
ecial Winter Lancashire Hot Pot • Six-Hour Braised Lam
 with Champ Potato • Hardwick Mutton • Lamb Birian
mb with Spinach • Black Lamb • Moroccan Lamb Tagin
amosa and Onion Bhaji • Slow Roast Shoulder of Lamb
 Lamb with Ginger and Chickpeas • Mint Lamb Chop
 Shallots and Spinach Mash • Special Winter Lancashir
 Six-Hour Braised Lamb Shoulder with Champ Potato
tton • Lamb Biriani • Rack of Lamb with Spinach • Blac

David Cameron by Tom Stoddart/Getty Images

My Hero
Lance-Corporal Johnson Beharry VC

Lance-Corporal Johnson Beharry VC epitomises the heroism of those who serve in our Armed Forces.

His book, *Barefoot Soldier*, tells a remarkable life story. He was born into grinding poverty and very difficult family circumstances. Large sections of *Barefoot Soldier* recount conversations with his grandmother in Grenada, whose constant encouragement told him he could make something of his life. He certainly didn't let her down.

After moving to England and joining the Army, he showed outstanding courage and selflessness. In particular, at the age of twenty-four, two extraordinary acts of heroism under fire in southern Iraq saved the lives of thirty comrades. The second left him in a coma from which few thought he would recover.

In 2005, he became the first living soldier to be awarded the Victoria Cross in decades. Wearing the medal makes Beharry happy not because it celebrates his own courage, but because it signifies that the colleagues he saved are living and well. That's the mark of a true hero.

And he hopes that other young people will see in his example a means to transform their own lives. Indeed his book ends with a great tribute to the power of heroes as role models. On his return to Grenada, his official motorcade slows down by a roundabout:

'I spot a group of small boys standing by the kerb. One of the kids, a boy of six or seven, steps forward. His T-shirt is torn; his feet are bare. He stands ramrod straight and snaps a salute. "Johnson Beharry!" he shouts. "I want to be you."'

Wearing the medal makes Beharry happy not because it celebrates his own courage, but because it signifies that the colleagues he saved are living and well.

Slow Roast Shoulder of Lamb

Ingredients

1 shoulder of lamb
6 cloves garlic, peeled
6 sprigs fresh rosemary
10ml olive oil
4 sprigs of fresh thyme
3 large carrots
3 leeks
3 sticks celery
8 cherry tomatoes
any other root vegetables you have lying around
2 x 400g tins chopped tomatoes
whole bottle red wine
1 bulb garlic, peeled
2 small dried red chillies

Method

Preheat the oven to180C / 350F / Gas Mark 4.

1 Pierce the lamb with a small knife several times to make a small hole, put a clove of garlic and half a sprig of rosemary in each slit and push right down.

2 Season the joint with salt and black pepper, and rub the olive oil all over. Put the thyme sprigs in the bottom of a casserole dish that has a lid and place the joint on top. Set aside for a moment.

3 Wash, peel and cut the carrots, leeks, celery and any other root vegetables you are using into large, bite-sized chunks. Put them and the tomatoes, over the lamb; then pour the red wine over the top.

4 Throw in the garlic (cloves separated) and crumble the chillies over the top.

5 Put the lid on the casserole and put it in the oven, after the first hour turn the oven down to 140C / 275F / Gas Mark 1 for the next 2½ hours.

6 After this time, remove the lamb from the oven, taking care not to splash the hot sauce over yourself. Taste and season the sauce before you serve.

7 Serve a couple of slices per person with the sauce and vegetables from the pot with your favorite potatoes. It's good, enjoy!!!

8 With (a lot of) thanks to Jamie Oliver for this dish.

DIFFICULTY LEVEL	PREPARATION TIME	COOKING TIME	SERVES
VERY EASY	10 MINUTES	3½ HOURS	4–6 DEPENDS ON JOINT SIZE

Captain Sally Durnford
Royal Army Medical Corps Physiotherapist

My Hero
Ernest Shackleton

Described as one of the 'finest leaders and greatest heroes of our time', Ernest Shackleton had already taken part in two Arctic expeditions when he published the famous advert with the opening line 'Men wanted ...' to walk across the Arctic.

The expedition set sail in December 1914 and all went well until eighty-five miles from the continent, where the Endurance became trapped in the unseasonably thick packed ice and slowly began to succumb to the crushing pressure. From here, Shackleton led his team for three hundred miles, pulling the loaded lifeboats overland, then a further hundred miles by sea to establish a camp on Elephant Island. He then selected a small team to travel onwards.

This team sailed eight hundred miles in an open twenty-two foot long lifeboat through some of the roughest seas of the southern hemisphere for seventeen days before making landfall on South Georgia where, despite frostbite, they walked the twenty-two miles across the island to alert the outside world to the plight of the rest of the team. This in itself represents a huge feat of human endurance and most of us would probably feel we had done as much as was expected of us by this

point. Not Shackleton. Over the following months he made repeated attempts to return to Elephant Island to rescue his team. Almost a full year after leaving Elephant Island, Shackleton returned to rescue them. Not a single man had been lost.

The fact that not a single life was lost over the whole two years of the expedition was in no small part due to Shackleton's inspirational leadership, his unwavering dedication to his men and the supreme loyalty and trust that Shackleton inspired in those he left on Elephant Island.

I first read this story as a little girl who never thought she would ever meet a hero, but over these last few years of 'conflict' that we have been involved in I have been constantly reminded that heroes do not need to be in Shackelton's mould – they are the brothers, sisters, fathers, mothers and friends of ordinary people and are around us every day. Extraordinary times make ordinary people into heroes.

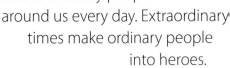

North African Lamb with Ginger and Chickpeas

DIFFICULTY LEVEL	PREPARATION TIME	COOKING TIME	SERVES
MODERATE	1 HOUR PLUS OVERNIGHT SOAKING	1¼ HOURS	4-6

Ingredients

170g dried chickpeas
2 large, firm aubergines
4 medium chillies
5cm-piece ginger
2 cloves garlic
10 fresh plum tomatoes
4 neck fillets of lamb (285g each)
1½ tbsp coriander seeds
½ tsp cumin seeds
¼ tsp grated nutmeg
4 tbsp olive oil
1 tsp vinegar
2 tbsp chopped fresh parsley
1 tbsp chopped fresh coriander

Method

1 Cover the chickpeas with cold water and leave to soak overnight.

2 The next morning, drain and rinse the chickpeas, put in a large sauce pan and cover with water. Bring to the boil and cook until tender (around 20–30 minutes). After this time drain and rinse in cold water.

3 Meanwhile cut the aubergines into one– inch cubes. Lay them out on a plate, sprinkle with one tbsp of salt (to remove the water) and leave for half an hour. Next, finely chop the chillies, ginger and garlic and set aside.

4 Cut a cross in the bottom of the tomatoes, plunge them into boiling water for one minute and put straight into iced water, remove the skins and cut into quarters and set aside.

5 Cut the lamb into two-inch pieces.

6 In a pestle and mortar grind the cumin and coriander with one teaspoon of salt; mix in the nutmeg and coat the lamb with the mixture.

7 Heat two tablespoons of the oil in a heavy based pan and cook the lamb until golden brown.

8 Sit a plate on top of the aubergines and gently squeeze out the excess water. Put in the pan with the rest of the oil, cook for two minutes, stirring continuously.

9 Add the chilli and ginger. Cook for a further three minutes, stirring.

10 Add the garlic and cook for one minute-keep stirring!!

11 Add the vinegar and tomatoes, turn the heat down to gently simmer, cover and cook for one hour, shaking the pan occasionally.

12 Add the chickpeas and cook, covered, for a further five minutes.

13 Gently stir in the parsley and coriander, taste the stew and season to your liking with salt and pepper.

14 Serve with cous cous (follow the cooking instructions on the packet).

My Hero
Isambard Kingdom Brunel

Isambard Kingdom Brunel was Britain's most accomplished engineer. He was a great innovator, and someone who believed that no problem is insurmountable.

His designs broke the mould, from the gravity-defying brilliance of the Royal Albert Bridge, to the ingenious network of viaducts and tunnels along the Great Western Railway. His legacy can still be seen all over the country.

But Brunel didn't stop there. He also built immense and impressive ships that were well ahead of their time, including the first steamship to make regular journeys across the Atlantic. During the Crimean War, Florence Nightingale famously raised the alarm over the filthy and dangerous conditions in the hospitals treating British soldiers. Never someone to shy away from a challenge, Brunel took on the task of helping these soldiers and designed a prefabricated hospital that was partly assembled in the United Kingdom and then shipped across to the injured forces. He took great care to create facilities with much higher standards of hygiene and sanitation, saving hundreds of soldiers' lives as a result.

Brunel was a man of great vision, whose boldness ignited the imagination of his Victorian peers, and whose work has continued to inspire generations since.

Mint Lamb Chops with Roasted Shallots and Spinach Mash

Ingredients

Lamb:
2 lamb chops
200g breadcrumbs
4 sprigs fresh mint
2 sprigs fresh parsley
100g flour
1 egg

Potatoes:
750g potatoes
75g spinach
25g butter
75ml milk

Shallots:
8 small shallots
50g butter
50g brown sugar

Mint Lamb Chops with Roasted Shallots and Spinach Mash

Method

1 Chop the mint and parsley and add to the breadcrumbs.

2 Put the breadcrumbs into one small bowl, flour into another, egg into another.

3 Now coat the lamb chops, first in the flour, then in the egg and finally in the bread crumbs.

4 Heat a frying pan to a medium heat. Add the oil and cook the chops for 3 minutes until golden brown, turn over and repeat.

5 Take off the heat and allow to rest for 3 minutes.

6 For the potatoes, put a pan of water on the stove to boil, peel and chop the potatoes and add to the water. Cook for 10–15 minutes until soft. Steam the spinach for 2 minutes, until they are wilted.

7 When the potatoes are soft, drain and put back into the saucepan, add the butter and mash the potatoes. Add the milk gradually, to prevent mash getting too soft. Season and fold in the spinach.

8 For the shallots, firstly peel them, then fry butter and sugar in a hot frying pan until golden brown.

9 Turn down the heat and cook for 2 minutes.

10 Now it is all ready to serve.

DIFFICULTY LEVEL	PREPARATION TIME	COOKING TIME	SERVES
MODERATE	30 MINUTES	20 MINUTES	2

My Hero
Tom Fletcher Mayson VC

Tom Mayson was an average young man from Cumbria who, one day in 1917, in three moments of bewildering heroism, earned the Victoria Cross. He reminds me why I care about history, and have the respect I do for the men and women who in the service of this country have been prepared to risk their lives for something they believe in.

31st July 1917 was the opening of the third battle of Ypres – later known as Passchendaele. The King's Own Royal Lancaster Regiment, which recruited many soldiers from the farms and villages that now make up my Barrow and Furness constituency, was one of many units that pushed the front line forward by a little over a mile that day – at the cost of some 32,000 men killed, wounded or missing.

When the King's Own Royal Lancasters were slowed by a German machine-gun post, Tom Mayson, 23-year-old lance-sergeant, shouldered his way into the ranks of the bravest ever to have worn the uniform. Charging forward, he disabled the machine-gun with grenades, wounding four Germans. Three escaped to a dug-out, but he followed and killed them. This reckless

determination was remarkable in itself, but Tom repeated it: later he charged another stubborn machine-gun post single-handed, killing six. Later, the Germans counter-attacked, and Tom, finding himself in charge of an isolated outpost, defended it successfully, only accepting the order to pull back when his ammunition ran out .

Staggeringly, Tom Mayson's was only one of fourteen VCs awarded that single day of terrible fighting. But Tom was a local man, and for me he sums up all the men who fought in that war, and the remarkable qualities of the British soldier. He died in Barrow in 1958 and is buried in St Mary's Church, Whicham, not far from the little village where he was born.

I'd cook Tom Mayson a Lancashire hot-pot. I'll bet he never ate anything nearly as warm and satisfying in the Flanders mud, and I'll bet he missed it.

Special Winter Lancashire Hot Pot

Ingredients

500g diced lamb
2 potatoes
3 carrots
1 small swede
1 leek
2 large onions
250 g pearl barley
1 bouquet garni (tea bag of bay leaf, thyme and parsley)
1 stock cube, lamb or beef
4 litres water
4 potatoes for the topping
50g butter for brushing the potatoes

Method

1 Dice the lamb and remove most of the fat.

2 Dice all the vegetables, except the potatoes for the topping.

3 In a frying pan, seal and brown the diced lamb.

4 Add onions and leek and saute for 5 minutes, until soft.

5 Add all other ingredients and bring to the boil.

6 Simmer until the lamb is tender, this will probably take about 2–3 hours.

7 While the stew is cooking, slice the potatoes for the topping.

8 Parboil in salted water for no more than 5 minutes.

9 Put the stew into an earthenware dish and overlap the potatoes over the stew.

10 Brush with melted butter and bake in a moderate oven for 30 minutes until the potatoes are brown.

DIFFICULTY LEVEL	PREPARATION TIME	COOKING TIME	SERVES
MODERATE	30 MINUTES	2-3 HOURS	4

Chris and James Tanner
Celebrity Chefs

My Hero
Our Dad

Our unsung hero has got to be our dad. When we were whippersnappers and working part time in restaurants it was Dad who ferried us around and picked us up at midnight every weekend. His encouragement and perfection for his chosen craft rubbed off on us and are crucial to our work to this day.

Our dad is a self-employed decorator; however, rollers and artex covering do not feature in his repertoire! He has prided himself with his bespoke skills: traditional paint methods and techniques, which are not widely seen these days. He knows more about paint and its chemical composition than most technicians. He gilded the gold leaf on the lions' heads at Buckingham Palace and has completed many restoration projects for English Heritage. His knowledge is exemplary but most importantly he is an unsung perfectionist. Attention to detail was always instilled in us as kids and this is one of the golden rules in our restaurants.

Without doubt he passed his genes for success on to us, and to watch him at work is a pleasure. We are two of four brothers and Dad's attitude, perfectionism and encouragement have shaped all of our futures. Although only two of us

have entered the wonderful world of gastronomy, our brothers have also proved successful in their chosen crafts. In Dad's words, 'If you want something go out and get it, don't expect it to drop in your lap.'

We could not have asked for a better dad and really appreciate that whilst we were growing up, although money was tight, we had a wonderful childhood. Dad loves his food and we're convinced he has hollow legs as he eats like a horse yet never weighs any more than twelve stone!

Our dad is a hero!

Six-Hour Slow Braised Lamb Shoulder and Champ Potato

Ingredients

1x2.2 kg shoulder of lamb
8 banana shallots
1 bulb garlic
10 sprigs thyme
250ml red wine
60g cold butter
3 large King Edward potatoes
3 spring onions
20ml milk
30g butter
1 large egg yolk

DIFFICULTY LEVEL	PREPARATION TIME	COOKING TIME	SERVES
EASY	10 MINUTES	5½ HOURS	2

126

Six-Hour Slow Braised Lamb Shoulder and Champ Potato

Method

1 Oil and season the meat. Peel the shallots and place in the tray with the meat in a hot oven of 180C / 350F / Gas Mark 4 for 30 minutes. Remove from the oven and drain off any fat, then turn down the heat to 120C / 250F / Gas Mark 1.

2 Peel the garlic and add to the meat with eight thyme sprigs. Cover with foil and cook for four hours and a half.

3 Next, pour over the red wine and cook for a further hour.

4 Remove from the oven and carefully put the lamb, garlic and shallots in a serving dish. Be careful, as it should be just falling off the bone.

5 Heat the cooking juices and skim off any fat, then whisk in the cold butter. Chop the remaining two thyme sprigs and stir in. Pour over the lamb and serve with champ mash.

7 For the champ, peel and chop the potatoes, boil in salted water until just soft.

8 Cut the tops off the spring onions and put in milk with the butter. Heat gently on the stovetop.

9 Drain and discard the spring onion tops.

10 Drain the potatoes and mash. Slowly mix in the milk mixture. Finely beat in the egg yolk.

Slice the onion bottoms and mix in. Serve with lamb shoulder.

Antony Worrall Thompson
Restaurateur and TV chef

My Hero
HRH Prince Charles

This man, our future king, has a great attitude to saving the planet, unfortunately the British press appear to knock everything he stands for and believe that as a future king he shouldn't have views on anything; they are so wrong. He has improved the lives of so many youngsters through The Prince's Trust, he has made people sit up and think about the planet through his passion for the organic movement. Not only does he think about it, he does it; his Duchy Range is a fine example of what can be done if you put your mind to it. Perhaps when he's King he won't be able to have these views which I for one would find disappointing. Personally I don't think we should have a cardboard

Photo by Mario Testino

cut-out sitting on the throne, there is no reason why there shouldn't be more interaction between the palace and the government. His enthusiasm for a better life inspired me to attempt in a small way life in a similar vein.

Herdwick Mutton with Creamy Onion Sauce and Buttery Mash
Ingredients

2 onions
8 cloves
2 stalks celery
2 carrots
2 turnips
3 kg leg of mutton
3½ litres lamb stock (or enough to cover the meat)
1 bouquet garni
salt

Sauce:
3 onions
4 sprigs parsley
55g unsalted butter
1½ litres white sauce, made with half milk and half lamb stock
vegetables from above
4 tbsp baby capers
300ml double cream

Perfect mash:
1 kg floury potatoes
115g unsalted butter
100ml full fat milk
4 tbsp double cream
½ tsp ground white pepper
1 level tsp salt

DIFFICULTY LEVEL	PREPARATION TIME	COOKING TIME	SERVES
MODERATE	30 MINUTES	DEPENDS ON THE SIZE OF THE JOINT	6–8

Herdwick Mutton with Creamy Onion Sauce and Buttery Mash

Method

1 Peel the onions and stud with the cloves. Roughly chop the celery, peel and dice the carrot and turnip.

2 Wipe the meat and trim off any surplus fat. Weigh the joint and allow 30–35 minutes per 400g plus an extra 30–35 minutes.

3 Put the mutton in the pan, cover with stock and add the bouquet garni and vegetables.

4 Bring to the boil, then reduce heat so that the water just murmurs and skim thoroughly from time to time throughout the cooking time. Boil for about 5 minutes to harden the outside of the meat, then reduce the heat and simmer gently. Season with salt when the mutton is half cooked.

5 Now for the sauce, finely chop the onions and finely chop the parsley.

6 Gently sweat the onions in the butter for 20 minutes, being careful not to brown them. Set them aside.

7 Pour white sauce into blender with the cooked vegetables and blend to a smooth liquid.

8 Pour onto the sweated onions, gently stir in the cream and finely add the capers and parsley, season to taste.

9 For the mash, peel and chop the potatoes, place into cold water with the salt and bring to the boil. Reduce the heat and simmer until tender.

10 Drain well in a colander, then return the potatoes to the pan and place over a gentle heat. Dry for a couple of minutes.

11 Mash with a traditional masher or ideally pass through a potato ricer.

12 Beat in the butter with a wooden spoon, and then gradually fold in the milk and cream, a little at a time. Season to taste.

13 Carve the meat, place on a serving dish and coat with onion and caper sauce. Serve with buttery mash. Do not over beat, or the mash will become sticky and elastic.

My Hero
Igor Ivor Sikorsky

Igor Ivor Sikorsky did not invent the helicopter but he did invent one of the very best helicopters – the Sea King, which first flew in 1959. This aircraft entered service with the Royal Navy in 1967 and has been used extensively in many different conflicts and in many varied roles ever since. Today, it is still at the forefront of helicopter operations helping to move and resupply British troops and evacuate wounded personnel in Afghanistan and Iraq.

In 1941 Sikorsky made the first helicopter flight that lasted over one hour in his Vought-Sikorsky VS-300. It used a three-bladed main propeller twenty-eight feet in diameter, and stayed in the air for 65 minutes and 14.5 seconds.

Helicopter Flown Successfully

WHAT is claimed to be the first successfully controlled vertical flight in a heavier-than-air machine was made recently by Ivor Sikorsky, prominent aeronautical engineer, at Bridgeport, Conn., in his new helicopter. Powered by a seventy-horsepower engine and equipped with variable-pitch rotor blades, the craft moved straight up from the ground for thirty feet, circled the field, and then settled vertically to the ground. Small rotor blades mounted on the bare fuselage of the craft act as elevators and rudder. Sikorsky is shown at the controls of the helicopter in the photograph.

Ivor Sikorsky about to take off on a test flight in his helicopter. At top, the odd machine in the air

AVIATION   POPULAR SCIENCE

He went on to pioneer the first stable, single-rotor, fully controllable helicopter to enter large full-scale production in 1942, upon which the majority of subsequent helicopters were based.

Lamb Biriani

Ingredients

400g lamb meat
1 large onion
2 good handfuls of chopped fresh spinach
200g basmati rice
4 tbsp balti curry paste
700ml lamb stock

Method

1 Remove all the fat from the lamb and cut into small cubes. On a different chopping board, slice the onion and roughly chop the spinach.

2 Wash the rice in cold water until the water runs clear and set aside.

3 Put the balti paste into a saucepan and cook over a medium heat until it sizzles and starts to release its flavors. Add the onion and cook until soft.

4 Add the lamb and cook for 5 minutes to seal the meat, this keeps in the juices.

5 Add the rice and stock, cover with a lid or cling film and cook over a very low heat for 15 minutes, or until all the liquid has been absorbed, stirring occasionally to prevent the rice sticking to the bottom of the pan.

6 Add the spinach and cook for 2 minutes to wilt.

7 Taste and season with salt and pepper.

8 Serve immediately with a warm naan bread.

Lamb Biriani

My Hero
Sir Tim Berners-Lee

Sir Tim Berners-Lee is the British scientist who single-handedly invented the World Wide Web. Whilst working in Geneva in 1990 he designed and let loose the protocol on which the entire World Wide Web is based to this day.

In 1994 he founded the World Wide Web Consortium (W3C) comprising various companies and foundations dedicated to improving the quality of the Web from both an engineering and humanist perspective.

Berners-Lee could quite easily be the richest man in history, were he to charge royalties for his invention. However, he more than anyone else has fought to keep the technology open, non-proprietary and free.

Ultimately, it is his commitment to the advancement of the global population through standardised and universal access to the vast collective knowledge repository of the World Wide Web that makes him my hero.

I would feed him this recipe because, in his honour, it is based on the first hit on Google when searching 'recipe+hero+spinach'. And because I like spinach!

Rack of Lamb with Spinach
Ingredients

600g new boiled potatoes
4 baby French-trimmed racks of lamb
(this can be done by any good butcher)
1 dash olive oil
200g baby shallots
4 rashers back bacon
200g fresh, washed spinach
4 tbsp creme fraiche

DIFFICULTY LEVEL	PREPARATION TIME	COOKING TIME	SERVES
MODERATE	20 MINUTES	30 MINUTES	4

Rack of Lamb with Spinach

Method

1 Pre-heat the oven to 200C / 400F / Gas Mark 6.

2 Boil the potatoes in their skins for about 10 minutes, rinse in cold water to cool quickly, slice into ½cm slices and set aside.

3 Sit the lamb in a roasting tin, season well with salt and pepper and rub the olive oil all over.

4 Roast the meat for 15–20 minutes for rare to medium and 25–30 minutes for well done.

5 Once cooked to your liking, remove from the oven and rest for about 10 minutes, covered with foil in a warm area.

6 Next, heat some vegetable oil in a frying pan and shallow fry the potatoes in batches to colour on both sides, season with salt, keep warm and set aside.

7 Meanwhile, heat a little olive oil in a frying pan, add the bacon and fry for 2 minutes, add the shallots, continue frying to crisp the bacon, stir in the spinach and cook until wilted, drain off any excess liquid, season with freshly ground black pepper and a little salt, as the bacon will already be salty.

8 To finish the dish, carve the lamb between the ribs into cutlets, arrange the bacon and spinach mix in the centre of four plates and top with the lamb cutlets. Finish the dish with a dollop of the creme fraiche on the side and garnish with the saute potatoes.

Serve immediately.

Squadron Leader Jon Pullen
RAF Engineer

My Hero
Edmund Blackadder

Edmund is a character who at each incarnation is a man who has been born with no advantage other than his own wit and intelligence. He is generally smart, charming and scheming and surrounded by sycophantic toadies who spend their time creeping up to whoever has influence. Edmund is my Hero for 2 reasons: Even against the odds, he always seems to come out on top through cynicism, charm and downright opportunism, but more importantly, he does so with a style and wit that is more cunning than a fox who has been appointed as professor of cunning at Oxford University.

Blackadder © BBC

Black Lamb
Ingredients

large shoulder of lamb
1 level tsp dry ginger
1 level tsp dry mustard
garlic salt
25g plain flour

Sauce:
1 small onion
30g melted butter
4 tbsp Worcestershire sauce
4 tbsp brown sauce
4 tbsp mushroom ketchup
2 level tbsp sugar
1 tbsp vinegar
140ml water

Method

1 Preheat oven to 220C / 425F / Gas Mark 7.

2 Trim excess fat from the lamb and weigh the joint. Season well with salt and pepper. Mix together the ginger, mustard and garlic salt, and rub well into the meat. Sprinkle the joint with the flour and put into a roasting tin.

3 Finely dice the onion, mix with all the other sauce ingredients and pour over.

4 Cook the joint in the oven for 30 minutes.

5 After this time, reduce the heat to 180C / 350F / Gas Mark 4 and continue cooking, allowing 30 minutes per 500g.

6 Baste the joint regularly and add more water if needed. (the joint will go very black, hence the name, do not worry you are doing nothing wrong).

7 Serve a couple of slices of the meat with creamy mashed potatoes and peas.

Black Lamb

DIFFICULTY LEVEL	PREPARATION TIME	COOKING TIME	SERVES
EASY	10 MINUTES	2½ HOURS	6 DEPENDS ON SIZE OF JOINT

My Hero
Blair 'Paddy' Mayne

Blair 'Paddy' Mayne is one of the founders of the Special Air Service (SAS). Each of his four citations reached the same conclusions as they described Mayne's qualities of superb, fine and brilliant leadership, as well as his outstanding gallantry. The DSO ranks just slightly lower in stature than the Victoria Cross and for Mayne to first gain that prestigious award while holding the junior rank of Lieutenant made it an even more significant achievement. The French Government held Mayne in very high esteem for his gallant and fearless conduct in helping to liberate their country from the Germans. They honoured him with the award of the Légion d'Honneur and Croix de Guerre on 5 March 1946 for his services. Those two great honours made him one of the most highly decorated Allied soldiers at the end of World War II.

Many of Mayne's principles and philosophies are still applied by the modern-day SAS. I would serve him Moroccan Lamb Tagine: Paddy spent a great deal of time in North Africa and it was reputed to be his favourite dish.

Lt Col Robert Blair 'Paddy' Mayne (MH 24415) by permission of the Imperial War Museum

Moroccan Lamb Tagine
Ingredients

10ml oil
1 cinnamon stick
1 tsp turmeric
2 tsp ground cumin
pinch of saffron
2 tsp dried coriander
2 tsp dried parsley
2 tsp dried mint
1 small onion
2–3 chillies
300g lamb (either neck or leg)
4 cloves garlic
230g can chopped tomatoes
2 tbsp honey
200–300ml lamb stock
4 dried apricots
20g fresh coriander
30g blanched almonds

Moroccan Lamb Tagine

DIFFICULTY LEVEL	PREPARATION TIME	COOKING TIME	SERVES
MODERATE	30 MINUTES	1½–2 HOURS	2

Method

1 Dice the lamb and remove most of the fat.

2 Mix together with all the dry herbs and spices and half of the oil. Marinade overnight, if possible.

3 Heat the remaining oil and cook the onion and chilli until soft.

4 Add the meat and garlic and cook for 2 minutes, until all the meat is sealed.

5 Add the tomatoes, honey and stock and cook for 1½–2 hours, until tender. This is best in the oven.

6 Add the apricots in the last 5 minutes of cooking.

7 Finely chop the coriander.

8 Remove the tagine from the heat and garnish with the almonds and fresh coriander.

9 Serve with either rice or cous-cous and naan bread.

My Hero

Earl Mountbatten of Burma

As the Supreme Allied Commander of South-East Asia Command (S.E.A.C.) (1943–1946) Louis Mountbatten was a truly charismatic figure. He cared about people, constantly boosting the morale of the troops under his command. For me it was the time he spent with the injured and desperately ill that I so admire him for. He was a champion of military hospital standards and would make every effort to ensure the hospital received what it needed for the best possible care of the injured. He was a tremendous encouragement not only to the patients but also to the staff. A great man who I had the privilege to meet when I was in charge of a ward for dangerously ill (DI) servicemen at the No14 British General Hospital in Rangoon.

At the end of the war I married a Burma Railway POW I had nursed at 14 BGH Rangoon – and if Louis Mountbatten had ever come to our home I would have loved to have served some really good Indian food to the man we referred to as 'the boss'.

by permission of the Imperial War Museum

Lamb Samosa & Onion Bhaji Served with a Mint Dressing

Ingredients

Samosas:
1 onion
2 cloves garlic
1½ tbsp fresh coriander
½ chilli (more if you like a bit more heat)
100g potatoes
small piece ginger
200g lamb mince
1 tsp garam masala
1 tsp black pepper
1 tsp poppy seeds
½ tsp chilli powder
1 tsp cumin
100g peas
10–12 pieces filo pastry

Bhaji:
4 large onions
8 cardamom pods
1 tsp chilli powder
1 tsp cumin
1 tsp ground coriander
1 tsp salt
1 tsp black pepper
1 tbsp oil
1 tsp vinegar
2 cloves garlic
small piece ginger
1 stalk mint
4 tbsp cornflour
2 tbsp plain flour
1 egg

Dressing:
500ml natural yogurt
2-3 stalks fresh mint
1 tbsp sugar

Lamb Samosa and Onion Bhaji Served with a Mint Dressing

Method

Samosas:

1 Finely chop the onions, chilli, potatoes and fresh coriander, then crush the garlic and ginger.

2 Fry the mince, add the chilli, onions, garlic and ginger and fry for a few minutes. Add all other ingredients except the peas; cook for about 20 minutes, add peas and leave to cool.

3 Brush a sheet of filo pastry with ghee or melted butter, fold in half lengthways and brush with butter again. Fold a short side up to the adjacent long side, fold the corner to the middle to create a small, triangular pocket. Put in a spoonful of the mixture before folding the rest of the sheet round the pocket, ensuring the mixture is sealed in. Brush again with butter.

Bhajis:

4 Quarter the onions, cutting from top to bottom, and slice very thinly.

5 Toast the spices in a dry frying pan for a minute or two, then add salt and pepper. Remove from heat and add the oil, vinegar and garlic and ginger to form a paste.

6 Mix the onions, paste, flour, corn flour, mint and egg together to form a stiff onion batter, chill for 2 hours.

7 Pre-heat a deep fryer to 160C / 320F. Fry the bhajis for 4 minutes so the centre cooks but the outside doesn't colour. Drain then rest.

8 Turn the fryer to 180C / 350F. Re-fry the bhajis until crisp and golden. Drain and serve.

Dressing:

9 Finely chop the mint and mix with the yogurt and sugar.

DIFFICULTY LEVEL	PREPARATION TIME	COOKING TIME	SERVES
MODERATE	30–45 MINUTES	5–10 MINUTES EACH	6–8

LIEUTENANT
AGNES HAMILTON

The Queen Alexandra's Imperial Military Nursing Service (QAIMNS) can trace its roots back to the Crimean War when Florence Nightingale was asked by the Secretary of State for War to take 38 nurses to the Barrack Hospital in Scutari, Constantinople, to nurse injured soldiers. In 1902 it was established by royal warrant when Queen Alexandra consented to become its first president.

By 1914, the QAs were well established and fulfilling a pivotal role in the Great War with approximately 100,000 nurses serving as far afield as Russia, East Africa, the Middle East and central Europe. This critical contribution continued into the Second World War where the QAIMNS grew from 640 nurses in 1939 to 12000 in 1945, providing medical and nursing care to servicemen and women across all theatres of war. One of these QAs was Lieutenant Agnes Hamilton.

Agnes had qualified as a State Registered Nurse in August 1940, specialising in orthopaedic nursing. Following in the footsteps of Jean, her younger sister, Agnes volunteered to join the QAIMNS and was posted to India, sailing on the SS Strathaird to Bombay. After some time working in a hospital in Kalyan

she was posted to the 128 Indian British General Hospital (IBGH) at Secunderabad in Hyderabad province where Burma Campaign casualties from the front line were treated. As well as the normal battle wounds, these service personnel often suffered from other more exotic ailments such as malaria, dysentery and other tropical diseases.

Unknown to Agnes at that time, a young British soldier by the name of Andrew Milliken from Walthamstow had already begun three and a half years captivity as a POW of the Japanese, working as one of the 60,000 Allied prisoners of war working on the Thai-Burma railway, grimly known as the Death Railway. The POWs lived in brutal conditions with very little sustenance and as a result over 16,000 of them lost their lives to the railway. By Christmas 1944 Andy Milliken had served his time on the building of the bridge on the River Kwai and was imprisoned in the Japanese POW camp at Hnong Pladuk.

The photos below capture the Christmas dinner celebrations of 1944 in the IBG hospital, where the patients and staff celebrated with a three-course meal offering a choice of roast turkey, goose or duck. In contrast, Andy Milliken and the other POWs of the Japanese celebrated their "White Christmas" with the same regular daily diet of unpolished rice washed down with boiled water.

As the Allied forces regained territory in South-east Asia, Agnes was posted to Chittagong and then to 14 British General Hospital, Rangoon. After the Japanese surrender in August 1945, POWs like Andy Milliken were brought to Rangoon where the QAs at the British General Hospital were the first women many of them had seen in four years. Andy the ailing POW was nursed back to health by Agnes; within 4 months they were married. That marriage lasted over 50 years until Andy died in 2001.

Today Agnes lives in a Christian home for the elderly in Ipswich.

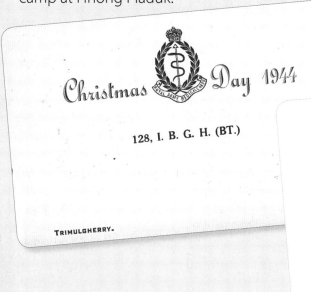

Christmas Day 1944

128, I. B. G. H. (BT.)

TRIMULGHERRY.

PATIENTS
Christmas Dinner

Cream of Tomato Soup

Roast Turkey

Roast Goose,
Bread Sauce,
Roast Potatoes,

Roast Duck,
Sausage Stuffing,
Cauliflowers or Peas.

Christmas Pudding
Brandy Sauce

Mince Pies
Beer

Fruit
Minerals

Nuts
Cigarettes

beef

...ch's Steak Dijon • Lasagne • Pickwick Pie • Fillet of Beef
...d Brioche • Tex Mex Spicy Balls • The Nimrod MR2 Hor...
...v • Steak, Ale and Mushroom Pie • Mince and Tatties •
...ellington • The Ultimate Roast Beef • Jack's Spa Boll • S...
...dney Pudding • Home-made Meatballs with Italian Sa...
... Mum's Beef and Guiness Casserole • Chequers Steak
...ch's Steak Dijon • Lasagne • Pickwick Pie • Fillet of Beef
...d Brioche • Tex Mex Spicy Balls • The Nimrod MR2 Hor...
...v • Steak, Ale and Mushroom Pie • Mince and Tatties •
...ellington • The Ultimate Roast Beef • Jack's Spa Boll • S...

Bruce Forsyth CBE
TV Presenter

My Hero
Sir Winston Churchill

Being just a child at the time of the Second World War, I developed an admiration for Sir Winston Churchill in our hour of need, and he certainly has to be my hero during my lifetime. The support he gave the British people at such a difficult time in our history is something everyone in this country should cherish. Thank God we had a man like that to help us through those terrifying days.

Forsyth's Steak Dijon
(as formerly served at the Wig and Pen Club, London)

Ingredients

1 thick, good quality sirloin steak
1 tbsp English mustard
1 tbsp Demerara sugar

Method

1 Cook both sides of the steak under a very hot grill, to your liking, three minutes each side for rare, four minutes each side for rare-medium and seven minutes each side for well done. (Taking into account the steak is going to go back under the grill)

2 On one side, spread the English mustard and sprinkle the sugar on top.

3 Put back under the grill, until the sugar starts to bubble and caramelise.

4 Serve with potatoes and vegetables of your choice.

I hope you enjoy it!

DIFFICULTY LEVEL	PREPARATION TIME	COOKING TIME	SERVES
VERY EASY	5 MINUTES	10 MINUTES	1

Forsyth's Steak Dijon
(as formerly served at the Wig and Pen Club, London)

Flight Lieutenant Michelle Goodman DFC
RAF Pilot

courtesy of Jon Enoch/The Times

My Hero
R2-D2

Being in the forces I meet brave and courageous people regularly, but for me the real heroes are the families that show unwavering support, love and understanding whilst their loved ones are on operations. My hero for the book, however, is going to be on a lighter note. I know this may seem odd, but I am a massive Star Wars buff. I have been told as a '70s child that you either watched Star Wars or Mary Poppins. Quite frankly a freaky baby-sitter who could turn into a helicopter with just a brolly was not my sort of thing. Out of all the characters in Star Wars, R2-D2 is my unsung hero; he is constantly saving the Rebels' lives and was instrumental in the defeat of both Death Stars. I think the Emperor's downfall was trying to seduce Luke to the dark side when really he should have been concentrating on the resourceful R2-D2. How a three-foot dustbin whose only weapon has the power of a 1.5V battery can defeat arguably the most evil villain in sci-fi history is a feat second to none. I would like to celebrate his bravery by sharing my lasagne with him and a mug of oil to swill it down.

Lasagne
Ingredients

2 litres milk
1 bay leaf
115g butter
115g plain flour
1 red onion
2 cloves garlic
4 rashers smoked bacon
1 tbsp olive oil
300g lean minced beef (tofu can be used for veggie lasagne)
2 tbsp tomato puree
6 tbsp Worcestershire sauce
400g can chopped tomatoes with herbs
175ml red wine
100g mushrooms
a handful of fresh chopped basil
20g butter
150g gruyere cheese
400g (no pre-cook) **lasagne sheets**

Method

1 Heat the milk gently with the bay leaf. Melt the butter, add flour, stir over a low heat for 2-3 minutes then gradually add the milk, stirring to make a smooth sauce, simmer gently for 10 minutes and season. Keep warm.

2 Finely dice the onion, crush the garlic and finely chop the bacon. Fry the onion and garlic in the oil for 2 minutes in a large saucepan, add the bacon and fry for another 2 minutes, then add the beef. Brown the meat and add the tomato puree, Worcestershire sauce and tinned tomatoes. Bring to the boil then add the red wine.

3 Cover it and simmer for 15 minutes, season and add more wine and Worcestershire if necessary.

Lasagne

DIFFICULTY LEVEL	PREPARATION TIME	COOKING TIME	SERVES
EASY	30 MINUTES	1 HOUR	4

4 Add the sliced mushrooms and basil, simmer again for 15 minutes.

5 Pre heat the oven to 200C / 400F / Gas Mark 6 and grease an ovenproof dish with the butter. Spread some meat mixture over the bottom of the dish, top with lasagne sheets, top with another layer of meat, then one of white sauce, then sprinkle with a little cheese.

6 Repeat these layers in the same order ending with lasagne coated with white sauce. The final coating is a layer of cheese.

7 Bake for 20–30 minutes until golden brown and bubbling, remove from the oven and leave to stand for 5 minutes.

8 Serve with salad and garlic bread.

FLIGHT LIEUTENANT
MICHELLE GOODMAN DFC

On the evening of 1st June 2007, Flight Lieutenant Michelle Goodman was the Captain of the Joint Helicopter Force (Iraq) Incident Response Team at the Contingency Operating Base at Basra Airport. The team is made up of a 3-man medical team, a 4-man RAF Regiment Aviation Reaction Force and a 4-man Merlin helicopter crew on 24-hour standby to respond to instant tasking. At 2315 hrs the team was alerted that there was a serious casualty following a mortar attack on an isolated British location in the centre of Basra City:

We were given the call quite late and by the time we knew of the task, we were already airborne. Basra city is only a couple of miles from our base at the airport so, before we knew it, we were on approach to the Landing Zone (LZ). Even from as far as 2 kilometres out the mortar flashes made it clear that the pick-up point was heavily under attack and that this wasn't going to be a routine lift.

For us, this was a new landing site that hadn't been used in a long time and accordingly it was thick with dirt and dust. It was down to Flight Lieutenant George Williams, the co-pilot on this trip, to do the amazing job of recognising the site amongst the broken urban sprawl of downtown Basra and getting us in on the correct approach.

As we descended, the dust cloud blew up to cut out visibility. Sergeant Chris Parker, the No 2 Crewman, was standing on the ramp at the rear providing situational awareness and watching out for flashes. As we descended to 20 feet, I lost all visibility and was relying entirely on Sergeant Steve Thomas, the No 1 Crewman, who by now was literally hanging out of the door to see the ground; he lost visibility with 10 feet to go leaving us 10 feet in the air under fire in an unknown landing site without any visible reference.

With great relief we got in first time; you are acutely aware in these situations that a second run could well be the difference between life and death and we had a young soldier with a head injury waiting for us. We were only on the ground for a couple of minutes. The Aviation Reaction Force left the aircraft and secured the site while the casualty was handed over to the on-board medical team who immediately got him on to the helicopter. From that point it was just a race to get him back to the hospital as quickly as possible.

On reflection, what was remarkable was how everybody just knew what to do. I guess it's the training kicking in, but we were a team that hadn't previously worked together and it all just clicked into place. At the time, it really didn't seem such a tricky operation; it was only when we got back and were debriefed that we knew that this trip had been sporty.

Michelle Goodman became the first female recipient of the Distinguished Flying Cross.

THE CITATION FOR HER AWARD READS:

Many IRT sorties are high risk. However, on this occasion Flight Lieutenant Goodman had to instantly weigh up the risks against the importance of recovering a serious casualty, which would impact on morale throughout the coalition. Without the IRT, the casualty would have died within 15 minutes. Despite extreme pressure, while in the face of the enemy, she made the right decision. This was a bold and daring sortie which undoubtedly saved life.

My Hero
Julius Caesar

There are many figures throughout history whom I would regard as iconic or pivotal in the course of human events: who might qualify, in my book at least, for 'hero' status. But there is one above all whom I find both hugely impressive and endlessly intriguing. Gaius Julius Caesar came from a patrician Roman family, of course. But his early life was far from a straightforward progression down a smooth path of privilege. In the political and sometimes deadly turmoil of the era he had to tread carefully and survive – quite literally at times – on his wits.

In later years he displayed the outstanding generalship and superb leadership qualities for which he is famed. But he also understood that lasting solutions in the territories over which he fought required political settlement as well as military success; a lesson that has great resonance today. He could – and did – think strategically, yet he also understood the concerns of the ordinary soldier. He was bold and decisive, but seldom rash and impulsive. He was, though, human, so not without faults. He was certainly ambitious politically, and many would regard his pursuit of power as a failing. More fatal to him, though, was the lack of subtlety he brought to that pursuit in his days as dictator – a lesson his heir, Octavian, learned well. But in death, as in life, Caesar did nothing in a small or forgettable way. And in his life and death he changed Rome, and with it the world.

There is some evidence to suggest that Caesar, like many Romans of his time, enjoyed the pleasures of the table. In choosing a dish for him, I decided that it was very appropriate for it to come from the furthest reaches of his conquests, and so here is a recipe for the quintessentially British Pickwick Pie.

Pickwick Pie

Ingredients

500g calves kidneys
4 medium white onions
90g butter
1.5 kg beefsteak (topside or rib eye)
plain flour for coating
250ml beef stock
¼ tsp powdered clove
¼ tsp marjoram
2 bay leaves
2 dessertspoons chopped parsley (fresh)
1 dessertspoon Worcestershire sauce
500g mushrooms
dash of olive oil
18 oysters
500g puff pastry
1 egg yolk
2 dessertspoons milk
150ml sherry (optional)
large bunch of parsley or watercress

DIFFICULTY LEVEL	PREPARATION TIME	COOKING TIME	SERVES
MODERATE	30 MINUTES	2 HOURS	8

Method

1 Soak kidneys in salt water for an hour and dice into medium-sized cubes.

2 Slice and saute the onions in butter until soft. Remove from the pan, keeping the butter.

3 Cut the beef into 3cm-square pieces, shake them and the kidney in a plastic bag containing plain flour, salt and pepper, to coat.

4 Saute the meat in batches in the butter, to a golden colour. Add the stock, herbs, spices and sauteed onions, stir thoroughly. Put into a heavy-lidded casserole and cook in a preheated oven at 140C / 275F / Gas Mark 1 for 1–1½ hours, until the meat is no longer chewy. Taste and season.

5 Saute the sliced mushrooms in the oil and season. Stir into the mixture with the Worcestershire sauce and put into a pie dish. If the gravy is thin, add a little flour mixed with cold water.

6 Lay the oysters on top. Put a pie funnel (or egg cup) in the centre of the dish. Roll the pastry evenly and place on top of the dish, trim off the excess and crimp the edges. Make a hole over the pie funnel to allow steam to escape.

7 Decorate with the leftover pastry and brush with an egg yolk and milk glaze.

8 Bake in pre-heated oven at 180C / 350F / Gas Mark 4 for 35 minutes, until golden brown and bubbling around the edge.

9 Just before serving, add sherry, if you wish, through the funnel hole and tuck in a bunch of watercress or parsley to decorate. Serve immediately.

Senior Aircraftman Adam Dover
RAF Chef

My Hero
Murielle Dover

My hero without a doubt is my wife Murielle, because she gave me a beautiful baby boy and kept me going when I was in Afghanistan. She told me about every new development straight away, and every new picture was sent. The love and devotion throughout my four-month tour was amazing. Even now her strength through tough times at home has been endless; she keeps us both going. That's why she is my hero, my drive and my lust for life.

I was deployed to Camp Bastian, Afghanistan in the summer of 2008. For one month of my four month tour I worked at the Forward Operational Base (FOB) which is basically out in a tent on your own feeding the lads that are out on dangerous operations, there is only 'compo' food (tinned and packaged, long life food) available to cook with at the FOB, no fresh ingredients at all, yes it's a challenge!

My best experience of this tour has to be using the Operational Field Catering System, (OFCS) which is the cooking equipment we use out in the field. We now have a new range of OFCS which has been in use for around 5 years and is much easier to use, safer and very well designed, however at the FOB you have to use the old kit and as you are out on your own you are quite segregated from all means of help and support should anything go wrong or any problems occur.

However you get a great sense of achievement when you have created a meal by yourself and with no fresh rations and when you see the appreciation from the Soldiers who have just returned from an operation and really need the hot food and atmosphere the mess tent provides, it makes it all worthwhile.

Fillet of Beef on a Toasted Brioche
with a Mushroom Duxelle with Courgette Ribbons and a Brandy Cream Sauce

DIFFICULTY LEVEL	PREPARATION TIME	COOKING TIME	SERVES
FAIRLY EASY	20 MINUTES	15–30 MINUTES	2

Ingredients

100g mushrooms
1 garlic clove
25g butter
1 sprig thyme
a little cream to bind
50ml brandy
200ml double cream
1 beef stock cube
2 tsp crushed black peppercorns
2 tbsp corn flour
2 courgettes
2 thick slices brioche bread
2 beef fillet steaks

Method

1 Slice the mushrooms and crush the garlic, fry in butter until soft. Add thyme leaves and cook for 2 minutes. Season and blend to a paste in a food processor. Add a little cream to bind.

2 Pour the brandy into a hot pan, boil to reduce by half, then add the cream. On a low heat, add the crumbled stock cube into the sauce and stir to dissolve. Add the peppercorns, and salt if required. Dissolve the corn flour in water and add gradually to thicken the sauce. Keep warm.

3 Peel the courgettes downwards with a vegetable peeler to make ribbons.

4 Quickly seal and brown the steaks in a little oil in a hot frying pan or griddle, season.. Then bake at 200C / 400F / Gas Mark 6 for 10–15 minutes for rare, 15–20 minutes for medium and 20–25 minutes for well done. Remove from oven and cover the steaks with foil to retain their heat and keep them moist.

5 Pan-fry the courgette ribbons in a little butter until soft. Toast both sides of brioches under a grill, spread with the mushroom duxelle and toast again to reheat.

6 To serve, put the brioche on a plate and top with the meat, garnish with the courgette and pour over the sauce at the last minute.

153

Stephen Ladyman, MP
MP for South Thanet; Vice Chair of the
Labour Party 2007-Present

My Hero
Donald Campbell

Donald Campbell is the only man to set land and water speed records in the same year. As a boy he was the ultimate hero to me – I could hardly imagine the bravery involved in breaking speed records, barely in control of the machine he was driving, and to do it time after time. To me he seemed super-human and indestructible, but sadly he wasn't. I was fourteen years old when he died and for days after his boat BlueBird crashed on Coniston Water, I expected him to be found alive – but as it slowly dawned on me that he had been mortal like the rest of us, my admiration for the way he had lived only increased.

Tex Mex Spicy Balls with Tomato Salsa

Ingredients

1 onion
500g mince
1 tsp Cayenne
1 tsp paprika
1 tsp black pepper
1 tsp ground spice
1 tsp chilli powder
1 egg
1 red pepper
3–4 tomatoes
1 red onion
3–4 chillies
1 bundle coriander
1 tbsp sugar
salt and pepper

Method

1 Preheat the oven to180C / 350F / Gas Mark 4.

2 Finely dice the onion.

3 Add the onion, all the spices, mince and egg into a bowl and mix together.

4 Roll into balls.

5 Put into the oven for 25–30 minutes.

6 Dice the red pepper, tomatoes and red onion. Finely chop the chillies and the coriander.

7 Put all together into a bowl. Add the sugar and season to taste.

8 Serve the balls on a bed of the sauce.

9 Serve with your favourite pasta.

Paul Allonby

Tex Mex Spicy Balls with Tomato Salsa

DIFFICULTY LEVEL	PREPARATION TIME	COOKING TIME	SERVES
MODERATE	20 MINUTES	25–30 MINUTES	4

Emma Parry
Co-Founder and Managing Director of Help for Heroes Trading Ltd

My Hero
Violette Szabo GC,

Women's Transport Service
(First Aid Nursing Yeomanry).

I was absolutely fixated by stories of the French Resistance and SOE agents when I was growing up, and my all time hero was Violette Szabo GC (the film "Carve her name with Pride" is still one of my all time favourite films). Violette Szabo was parachuted into France in April, 1944, and was twice arrested by the Germans but each time managed to get away. Eventually, however, with other members of her group, she was surrounded by the Gestapo in a house in the south west of France. Resistance appeared hopeless but Violette, seizing a Sten-gun and as much ammunition as she could carry, barricaded herself in part of the house and, exchanging shot for shot with the enemy, killed or wounded several of them. By constant movement, she avoided being cornered and fought until she dropped exhausted. She was arrested and had to undergo solitary confinement. She was then continuously and atrociously tortured but never by word or deed gave away any of her acquaintances or told the enemy anything of any value. Eventually she was sent to a concentration camp and was ultimately killed by firing squad.

On 17 December 1946, her daughter Tania, aged 4, went to Buckingham Palace to receive her mother's posthumous George Cross from King George VI.

courtesy of the Violette Szabo Museum. www.violette-szabo-museum.co.uk

Hero Pie
Ingredients

700g stewing steak
4 tbsp plain flour
salt and pepper
3 tbsp oil
2 large onions
225g field mushrooms
150ml beef stock
285ml ale
good splash of Worcestershire sauce
1 packet ready-made puff pastry
1 egg beaten

Hero Pie

Method

1 Preheat oven to 160C / 325F / Gas Mark 3.

2 Cut the meat into one-inch pieces.

3 Cut the onions into large dice and cut the mushrooms in half.

4 Roll the meat in the seasoned flour.

5 Heat a large casserole dish with a lid, add oil and fry the meat in batches until brown on all sides.

6 Add the onions and fry gently for about 10 minutes, adding more oil if necessary.

7 Add the Worcestershire sauce, stock, ale and some salt and pepper. Give it all a really good stir and bring to the boil.

8 Put the lid on and transfer to a moderate oven for around 2 hours, or until the meat is tender.

9 Add the mushrooms half way through and check the seasoning.

10 When the meat is cooked, transfer to a pie dish and allow to cool.

11 Increase the oven temperature to 200C / 400F / Gas Mark 6.

12 Roll out the pastry to fit the dish and place on top (decorate if you are feeling artistic!), and then make a slit in the middle for the steam to escape.

13 Brush lightly with the beaten egg and cook for around 20–25 minutes in a hot oven until golden.

14 Serve with a good dollop of mashed potatoes and seasonal vegetables.

DIFFICULTY LEVEL	PREPARATION TIME	COOKING TIME	SERVES
MODERATE	20 MINUTES	2 HOURS 25 MINUTES	6

Wing Commander Mark Gilligan
RAF Engineering Officer

My Hero
Billy Connolly

Regardless of the circumstances of my life, I have come to the conclusion that the one thing that gets me through the most stressful and difficult of times is humour. I think it's fair to say that the humour of the armed forces is slightly different to that of mainstream society; it's a unique form of black humour prompted by the often bleak environments and events in which we find ourselves involved. Perversely, when things are at their most serious you often find people at their least serious! I also find that the appropriate application of humour bonds a team together and can make the vital difference between achievement and failure. So I admire those who can create humour out of the apparently mundane.

My hero is Billy Connolly. The guy is a genius who has maintained a standard that hasn't flagged in the almost forty years that I've been laughing at his particular views of life. I remember as an eighteen-year-old, sitting in the lounge of my aunt's house in Chardon, Ohio, laughing to the point of causing myself physical discomfort (or social embarrassment) while listening to his version of the crucifixion with an American girl who was as bemused as I was amused, because she didn't understand a word of it.

Basically, I aspire to be as windswept and interesting as him! How much fun would it be to have dinner with Billy Connolly? I've decided that I'd cook him Boeuf à L'Ecosse and Creamed Potatoes (mince and tatties) for two reasons: firstly, I'm sure it would remind him of his childhood in Glasgow and would no doubt prompt some trademark humour, and secondly, because it's the only hot meal I know how to cook from first principles!

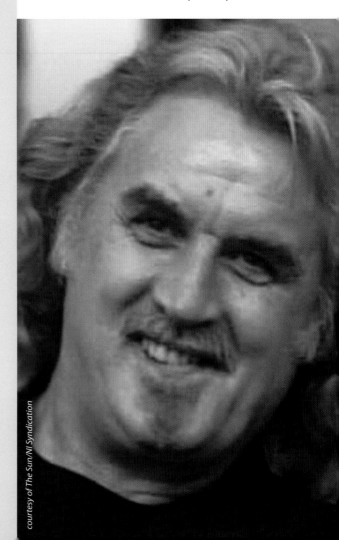

courtesy of The Sun/NI Syndication

Mince and Tatties

Ingredients

800g lean minced beef
1 large onion
2–3 large cloves garlic
olive oil
8 tbsp brown sauce
4 tbsp tomato sauce
2 tbsp Worcestershire sauce
450ml beef stock
seasoning

Method

1 Brown the mince in a pan containing olive oil, salt and pepper.

2 Finely chop the onion and garlic and soften on a low heat in a separate pan.

3 When the mince is brown, add the onion garlic and stock. Bring to the boil and then reduce the heat to simmer.

4 Add the brown, red and Worcestershire sauces and season to taste.

5 Serve with mashed potatoes.

DIFFICULTY LEVEL	PREPARATION TIME	COOKING TIME	SERVES
EASY	20 MINUTES	30 MINUTES	4

My Hero
Sir Ian Botham

My hero is Sir Ian Botham. I am not a great cricket fan but Ian's heroics for the England team in the Ashes test series match against Australia in 1981 are the stuff of sporting legend. However, it is not for his sporting prowess that I chose Ian; it is for his phenomenal feats of fundraising for Leukaemia Research. There are far easier ways of fundraising for charity than the twelve long-distance walks around Great Britain that Ian has completed. I have had the pleasure of accompanying him on some of his walks and the experience is always uplifting. Ian doesn't walk slowly – he almost sprints – and even in my racing chair it's hard to keep up with him. At the end of each day he may be exhausted, his feet blistered and bleeding, but his mind is always focused on the charity he is supporting. So far he has raised over ten million pounds, an amazing feat from a remarkable man.

courtesy of The Sun/NI Syndication

Beef Wellington
Ingredients

1.5 kg beef fillet
salt
black pepper
2 tbsp sunflower oil
45g butter
1 small onion
250g flat mushrooms
175g smooth liver pate
400g ready-made puff pastry
1 egg

Method

1 Trim the beef and remove any sinews. Season with black pepper, heat the oil in a frying pan, add the beef and cook on high, until browned all over.

2 Finely chop the onion and mushrooms. Melt the butter in the frying pan, add the onion and mushrooms and cook until softened. Put all this in bowl and leave to cool. Add the liver pate to the onion and mushroom mix. Add salt and pepper to taste.

3 Roll out the pastry to a rectangle roughly 30x40 cm, spread half the pate mix down the middle. Place the beef on the pate, cover with the remaining pate, fold the pastry over to form a parcel, glaze with the beaten egg.

4 Bake at 220C / 425F / Gas Mark 7 for 30–45 minutes, depending how rare you like your meat. Cover with foil for last 15 minutes to prevent the pastry becoming too brown. Leave to stand for 10 minutes, then slice and serve.

Beef Wellington

DIFFICULTY LEVEL	PREPARATION TIME	COOKING TIME	SERVES
MODERATE	20 MINUTES	30 MINUTES	8

My Hero

Admiral of the Fleet Sir Michael Le Fanu GCB DSC

He was already a legend in the Navy but I first came across Michael Le Fanu in 1951 when he was Captain of the 3rd Training Squadron, undertaking anti-submarine activities. He was a very popular man – terribly humorous but also with exacting standards. I was the Engineering Officer of HMS Creole, part of his squadron. One day we were out on exercises – he was embarked in our sister ship HMS Crispin. We had been out all day and it was time to return to port, and as we turned for home he sent a signal to us saying 'last one home's a sissy'. Needless to say we both upped revs to try to beat each other back – and kept perfect station on each other all the way home. For some reason he took a bit of a shine to me and a few weeks later he sent another signal: 'Captain D to Donald: I am not God and you are not Moses'. Well, I had no idea what to make of it but knew I was expected to reply. So I called for a Bible and sat in the Engine Room poring over the text trying to think what to write, and persuaded the Commanding Officer to allow me to send 'Engineering Officer to Captain D: You may not be God and I may not be Moses

but there is enough bull in this ship to rush anywhere'. A few years later he made Admiral and I came across him again, this time in the Admiralty in London. The office in which I worked was right next to the building's incinerator, which of course used to belch smoke when lit. Imagine my surprise when, a few weeks after arriving in post I received a signal 'Le Fanu to Keable: Stop making black smoke'. Of course in those days it was still a mortal sin for ships to make smoke – this made you an easy and visible target for submarines. It was things like that which people remembered him for and are examples of his style: he was a brilliant leader who personalised things. Don't get me wrong, he had an iron core but he also had a softer edge, and as a result he was hugely respected and anyone would do anything for him. Who else would issue all his orders in riddles?! We adored him and missed him terribly after his death.

Admiral of the Fleet, Admiral Le Fanu (MH 3086) by permission of the Imperial War Museum

The Ultimate Roast Beef and Yorkshire Pudding

Ingredients

**fore rib of beef (about 4 kg),
  trimmed, boned and rolled.**
olive oil
wholegrain mustard
salt
freshly cracked black pepper
3 eggs
115g flour
salt
275ml milk
beef dripping or lard

Method

1 Rub the beef all over with the olive oil, wholegrain mustard, salt and pepper.

2 Put a heavy-based roasting tray on the hob over a high heat. When hot, put the beef in and seal on all sides to colour and crisp the outside.

3 Put the beef immediately into the oven, pre-heated to its highest setting, for 20 minutes.

4 Reduce the heat to 190C / 375F / Gas Mark 5 and roast for 30 minutes per kilo for rare, add another 10 / 20 / 30 minutes per kilo for medium rare / medium / well done.

5 Remove and place on a board or tray, loosely cover with foil and rest the meat for a minimum of 40 minutes.

6 Mix the eggs and flour with a pinch of salt, add the milk gradually, whisking to a runny batter. Leave to rest, covered, in the refrigerator.

7 Put 1cm of beef dripping or lard in the bottom of baking moulds or tin and heat in the oven, at maximum temperature, for 5–10 minutes, until smoking hot.

8 Whisk the batter again, pour into the moulds or tin and bake for around 25 minutes until golden brown and crispy (don't open the oven door for the first 20 minutes).

9 Serve immediately with the carved beef, horseradish sauce, crisp roast potatoes and thick beef gravy.

DIFFICULTY LEVEL	PREPARATION TIME	COOKING TIME	SERVES
EASY	20 MINUTES	1½ HOUR	6-8

Flight Sergeant Paul Quinlan
RAF Senior Non-Commissioned Officer

My Hero
My son Jack

Jack was born with a cleft lip and palate and has undergone numerous operations since. It was during recovery from one of these operations, having just had a bone graft from his leg into his mouth, that all the alarms went off at 1 a.m., sending the nurses running, as Jack's heart rate dipped below 25 bpm. Many tests and more sleepless nights led to the diagnosis of a heart block – where electrical impulses do not pass properly between the sections of the heart, and sometimes do not pass at all. At the age of twelve Jack was fitted with a pacemaker as a precautionary measure. As if operations on his lip, palate, ears, leg and heart were not enough, he has also broken both arms at the same time and been through the biggest break of all: the divorce of his parents. Throughout all this, he has never ceased to amaze me with his ability to take everything in stride. When he had his pacemaker fitted his mother and I were worried sick, and, after all the operations he had had, we just felt he had been through enough and were struggling to keep it together. Jack walked up to his mum, gave her a hug and simply said, 'Don't worry, Mum, I'll be fine'; he was still smiling encouragement and joking as the anaesthetist put him under. Now thirteen, he has grown into a loving, intelligent lad with a sharp brain and cheeky wit, a love of the outdoors and animals and something of an incomprehension for people who do not appreciate what a wonderful world is around them and treat it, and others, badly.

But most of all, he holds a philosophy that many of us, who will go through far less in our lifetime than he has done in his few years, have lost sight of as we drift automaton-like through our daily routine. We were walking up a hill several years ago, enjoying the day, and he turned to me with a serious look on his face. 'Do you know what?' he asked. 'I think that life is an adventure, and you've just got to go out there and enjoy it.' He turned and walked on; I stopped, dumbfounded by a ten-year-old.

Jack's Spaghetti Bolognese

Jack's favourite meal is Spaghetti Bolognaise. I know what you are thinking: "Spa Boll? Fry some mince, add a jar of Ragu, 20 minutes, done." Not quite. The better the quality of ingredients you use here, the better it is going to taste, and it has to cook for at least 2 hours. If you're going to cook for someone you love, cook it with love.

The better the quality of ingredients you use here, the better it is going to taste, and it has to cook for at least 2 hours. If you're going to cook for someone you love, cook it with love.

Jack's Spaghetti Bolognese

Ingredients

olive oil
1 large onion
2–4 cloves garlic, according to your taste
2x400g tins plum tomatoes (not the chopped ones)
red wine
dried mixed herbs
balsamic vinegar
red wine vinegar
Worcestershire sauce
tomato ketchup or puree
fresh ground black pepper
450g beef mince
one-inch thick chunk of pancetta, diced
Shitake mushrooms
1 large egg and 100g of tipo 00 pizza flour per person
block of Parmigiano Reggiano to serve

Method

1 Finely chop the onion and garlic, fry lightly in olive oil in a large frying pan, until the onions become soft and transparent without colouring.

2 Add the tomatoes and one of their tins about two-thirds full of red wine. Add the herbs, the balsamic and red wine vinegar, some Worcestershire sauce, ketchup or puree and, finally, freshly ground black pepper. (Up to you how much of all these to add – you can adjust the quantities later when you taste it – but don't be shy!)

3 Bring to boiling point and allow to reduce slightly.

4 While the sauce is reducing, fry the pancetta in a dry frying pan, and then fry the beef in its fat – don't overload the pan. Use quite a high heat and don't worry if some bits get a little burnt.

Add a little olive oil before frying subsequent batches, if necessary.

5 Add the meat to the sauce and simmer for 1–1½ hours, covering part of the time so it reduces gently.

6 Taste after an hour and add more of the sauce ingredients if necessary. Break up any large pieces of tomato.

7 Add the cleaned, roughly broken up, mushrooms an hour before serving.

8 Simmer for another hour or so, until the sauce is thick but not dried up (again cover part of the time if necessary).

9 Add salt, (or a little light soy sauce) to taste.

10 Mix the eggs and flour in a food processor to resemble breadcrumbs. Shape into a ball, put into a lightly floured bowl, cover with cling film and refrigerate for around half an hour.

11 Roll and cut it using a pasta machine (or a very large rolling pin and a sharp knife).

12 Boil a large pan of salted water, add the pasta, stir once and return to the boil. It should take 1½–2 minutes to cook (fish out a bit and try it!).

13 Drain and add to the sauce, mix well and serve with the freshly grated Parmigiano Reggiano.

14 To accompany it, a Caesar salad is excellent, or, if your name is Jack, annoy your dad, after all his hard work, by squirting loads of extra tomato ketchup over the top!

DIFFICULTY LEVEL	PREPARATION TIME	COOKING TIME	SERVES
MODERATE	1 HOUR	2–3 HOURS	4-6

John Prior
Royal Navy Veteran

My Hero
Private Frederick Lacey
Notts & Derby Regiment

Private Lacey was my dad's best friend and they volunteered to join up together prior to hostilities in 1939. Dad joined the RAF but Freddie was not accepted, and decided instead to join the Army. Freddie was captured at the fall of Singapore and was interned by the Japanese. On 12 September 1944 Freddie was being transported to Japan with other POWs when the ship carrying them was sunk by American aircraft. Freddie did not survive the attack and died aged twenty-five. I was born a year later and was christened John Frederick Lacey Prior in memory of Freddie. Although I never met Freddie, he has always been my hero because I feel that he died so that I might live in peace and freedom.

Fred Lacey pictured right with John's dad (centre)

Steak and Kidney Pudding
Ingredients

500g rump steak
120g ox kidney
7g parsley
90g onions
250ml cold brown stock (made from stock cubes or made fresh if you wish)
240g flour
1tsp baking powder
110g shredded suet
¼ tsp salt
60ml water

DIFFICULTY LEVEL	PREPARATION TIME	COOKING TIME	SERVES
MODERATE	15 MINUTES	UP TO 3½ HOURS	4

Method

1 Trim the meat of all fat and cut into small dice. Skin the kidney, if not already done, and cut it into same small dice. Put all this into a large bowl.

2 Chop the onions into the same size dice, and add to the meat. Finely chop the parsley, add to the meat mix, and stir thoroughly. Cover with the cold stock, season well with salt and pepper and allow this to stand while you make the pastry.

3 To make the suet paste, sieve the flour and baking powder into a large bowl, add the salt and the suet and stir to combine. Add the water to make a paste. Roll the pastry out to a quarter of an inch thickness and line either 4 small basins (dariole) or one large basin of a suitable size. (Ensure you leave enough pastry for a lid or lids).

Steak and Kidney Pudding

4 Put the meat mixture into the lined basin(s). Wet the edges and cover with the lid(s). Press these down firmly.

5 Damp a tea-towel in hot water, wring out and tie around the basins, allowing enough room for the pastry to expand.

6 If you are making a large pudding, steam for 3½ hours or, for the smaller ones, 2 hours.

7 Turn out, being careful not to get any water on the puddings.

8 Serve immediately with mashed potatoes, vegetables and thick homemade gravy.

Major Jake Little MC
Yorkshire Regiment Officer

My Hero
Sir Ranulph Fiennes

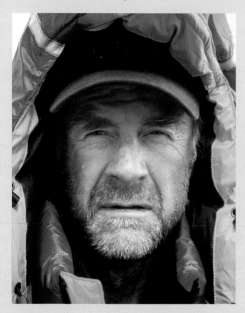

An old-fashioned British hero who has continuously risked all to explore both geographically and the limits of the human body, Fiennes is described as 'the world's greatest living explorer' by the Guinness Book of Records. In 1993 Queen Elizabeth awarded Fiennes with the Order of the British Empire (OBE) for 'human endeavour and charitable services' because, on the way to breaking records, finding lost cities, crossing continents and circumnavigating the globe, Sir Ranulph has raised over £5 million for charity. It would take all day to list his achievements but I think most significant is the example he sets to us all in overcoming personal tragedy and illness.

Home-made Meatballs with an Italian Sauce and Pasta

Ingredients

1 onion
1 kg tomatoes
2 cloves garlic
olive oil
fresh basil
balsamic vinegar
80g grated cheese (Parmesan or similar)
500g minced beef
50g dried breadcrumbs
50g skinless sausage (Mortadella or salami)
1 egg
fresh parsley
milk
80g per person of spaghetti or any other of your favourite pastas

Method

1 First prepare your vegetables: finely dice the onion and skin the tomatoes by putting into boiling water for 20 seconds, then plunge into iced water. Remove the skins, then cut into a rough chop, crush the garlic.

2 Fry the onion gently in a little of the oil, add the tomatoes and throw in a good handful of chopped basil and a splash of the balsamic. Bring to the boil and simmer gently for 30 minutes.

3 In a large bowl, mix the garlic, cheese, mince, breadcrumbs, sausage, egg, a good handful of finely chopped parsley and more finely chopped basil. Season well with salt and pepper, and, if needed, add a little milk to make the mixture soft.

4 Form the mince mixture into golf-ball-size balls and brown in a frying pan, in batches if necessary.

Home-made Meatballs with an Italian Sauce and Pasta

5 Transfer the meatballs to the sauce and simmer for 10 minutes.

6 Taste and season to your taste, if needed.

7 Serve with your hot pasta and a generous dusting of Parmesan

DIFFICULTY LEVEL	PREPARATION TIME	COOKING TIME	SERVES
EASY	25 MINUTES	45 MINUTES	4–6

Ewan McGregor
Actor

My Hero
Jimmy Stewart

Jimmy Stewart was an American film and stage actor best known for his unpretentious persona. Over the course of his career, he starred in many films now widely considered classics, and was nominated for five Academy Awards, winning one whilst also receiving a Lifetime Achievement Award. What many people don't know is that he also had a noted military career, rising to the rank of Brigadier General in the United States Air Force Reserve.

Mum's Beef and Guinness Casserole

Ingredients

900g casserole steak
1 large onion
1 red pepper
25g butter
25g flour
1 tbsp tomato puree
½ can Guinness
500ml beef stock (made fresh or with stock cubes)

Method

1 Dice the steak into medium-sized cubes then, on a different chopping board, cut the pepper and onion to the same size.

2 Fry the onion and pepper in the butter in a large saucepan until soft, transfer this mix, using a slotted spoon, into a large casserole dish.

3 Next, in the same saucepan, fry the steak until brown, season with salt and pepper, then using a slotted spoon transfer and mix into the onion and red pepper.

4 Put the saucepan back on the heat to heat the juices left and then add the flour to make a roux. Cook for a few minutes over a low heat, stirring all the time, add the tomato puree, mix in, then pour over the Guinness, stir in and add the beef stock, a little at a time, stirring all the time to make a smooth sauce. Taste and season to your liking.

5 Pour the sauce over the meat mix; put the lid on the casserole dish and cook in the oven at 170C /325F / Gas Mark 3 for about an hour.

6 Stir the casserole and serve (at Ewan's request) over creamy, piping hot mash!!

Mum's Beef and Guinness Casserole

DIFFICULTY LEVEL	PREPARATION TIME	COOKING TIME	SERVES
EASY	15 MINUTES	1 HOUR	4

Gordon Brown MP
Prime Minister

My Hero
Eric Liddell

Most people have heard of Eric Liddell for his sporting exploits, representing Great Britain in athletics and Scotland in rugby in the 1920s. He famously refused to run on a Sunday at the 1924 Paris Olympics, giving up the chance of a medal in the 100 metres, only to go on and clinch gold and the world record in the 400 metres, events immortalised in the film *Chariots of Fire*. He gained his sporting fame at Edinburgh University, and if the food was the same as it was in my days there, he would have approved of hearty fare like the Chequers Pie. But to my mind, it was through his lesser-known exploits after leaving Edinburgh that he truly proved himself a hero. He returned to China – the land of his birth – to take over his father's missionary work, and married a Canadian nurse. When Japan invaded Northern China, he continued his work, even when it became too dangerous for his wife and daughters to stay in the country. In 1943, along with other remaining Westerners, he was placed in an internment camp. With his customary energy and selflessness, he organised activities for the interns throughout the week and school for their children on Sundays. Illness eventually struck him down, and he died in captivity just a few

months before the war's end. Every memoir written by his fellow interns records his kindness and inspiration throughout those dark days of war. No trace of the camp remains. Just a memorial stone made of Scottish granite, bearing this inscription from Isaiah: 'They shall mount up with wings as eagles; they shall run and not be weary.'

Chequers Steak Pie

Ingredients

800g beef chuck steak
100g oil
100g flour
1 litre hot beef stock
1 large onion
1 carrot
1 leek
Worcestershire sauce
1 bay leaf
200g puff pastry
1 beaten egg

If you wish to make this pie in advance, stop before you top the pie, cool slightly at room temperature before putting in the fridge until you are going to use it. It can also be frozen, once cool, for up to 4 weeks.

Chequers Steak Pie

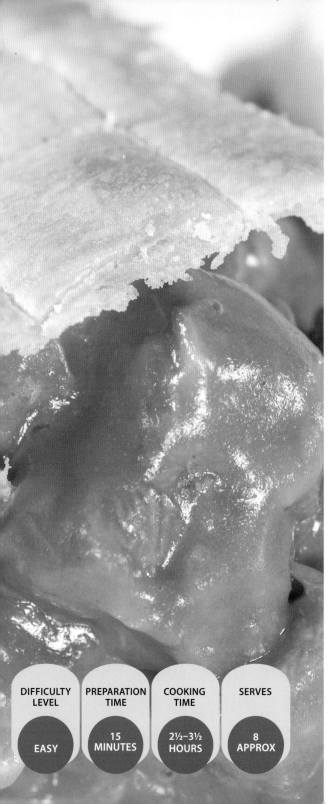

Method

1 Trim the beef and cut it into 1 inch squares. On the hob, heat the oil in a deep pan (a hob-proof casserole dish is perfect) and brown the beef on all sides, seasoning with salt and pepper as you go. When brown on all sides remove the beef from the pan.

2 Dice the onion into small cubes and fry it in the same pan until soft.

3 Add the flour to make a roux. Slowly add the stock, a little at a time, stirring continuously to make a smooth sauce.

4 Return the beef to the pan; add the bay leaf and season with salt, pepper and Worcestershire sauce to taste.

5 Wash the leek and celery and peel the carrot and add them whole to pan, stir the sauce, cover with a lid and cook slowly in the oven on a moderate heat around 160C / 325F / Gas Mark 3, until the meat is tender.

6 When the meat is tender, remove the carrot, celery and leek, taste and add more seasoning if required.

7 Put the mixture in a suitable pie dish, set aside, roll out the pastry to fit the dish and place on top, crimp the sides if you wish.

8 Brush the pastry with the beaten egg, put in a hot oven, 200C / 400F / Gas Mark 6 until the pastry is golden brown, around 20–30 minutes.

9 Serve immediately with your choice of potatoes and vegetables.

DIFFICULTY LEVEL	PREPARATION TIME	COOKING TIME	SERVES
EASY	15 MINUTES	2½–3½ HOURS	8 APPROX

The RAF Nimrod Fleet

My Hero
The Rescue Services

The Rescue Services are both military and civilians who are prepared to put their lives at risk to help, assist and save the lives of others in distress.

In total, there were 2,065 call-outs attended in 2007 by RAF and Navy Helicopters, Nimrod aircraft and Mountain Rescue Teams (MRTs), assisting some 1817 individuals; 48% of these were to Scotland, the South West region or Wales; a further 32% of call-outs were out to sea. To this, the MRTs contributed some 102 call-outs, assisting 41 persons. Finally, Coastguard helicopters added a further 220 call-outs, assisting a further 618 persons to these totals.

The Nimrod MR2 Honkers Stew

Ingredients

2 tins compo stewed steak
1 tin compo sausages
1 large tin compo baked beans
1 large tin compo boiled new potatoes
1 tin compo carrots
1 tin compo pear halves in syrup
sliced white bread
2 tsp medium curry powder
½ cup strong black coffee
tomato ketchup
salt and pepper to taste.

Method

1 Add both tins of stewed steak to a warm pan, stir to release gravy.

2 Add curry powder ketchup and coffee, stir gently.

3 Slice the compo sausages into even pieces and add to pan.

4 Chop the new potatoes and carrots into even pieces and add to pan.

5 Add the baked beans and heat gently, stirring regularly until warm through.

6 Just before serving, add the chopped pear halves and mix in.

7 Serve immediately with lots of white sliced bread and wash down with hot strong tea. Lovely!

DIFFICULTY LEVEL	PREPARATION TIME	COOKING TIME	SERVES
EASY	20 MINUTES	5 MINUTES	6–8

The RAF Nimrod Fleet

The following script is based on a typical real-life scenario, some 150 miles to the west of Scotland and in the very early hours of a stormy winter's morning. A Nimrod aircraft is airborne, 'scrambled' some two hours earlier to locate a fishing boat with an injured sailor onboard; a RAF Sea King helicopter was already airborne although, slower and with less endurance, it had already been forced to refuel en route to the scene. Far from the Scottish coast, the Sea King pilot is relying on the Nimrod to provide a safety watch (known as Top Cover) over his transit to and from the vessel, as well as locating it, relaying the exact position so that he doesn't have to waste valuable time and fuel searching. The author is onboard the Nimrod aircraft:

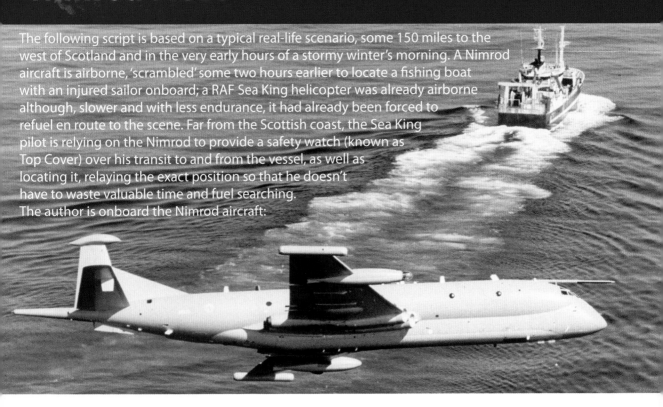

'Rescue 137, this is Rescue 51, you have 55 miles to run to the fisher, the southerly of 3 lying NE/SW, the skipper is expecting you on-top at 0532 Zulu, to call him on Channel 16 to arrange the lift.'

'Rescue 51, Rescue 137, copied. Will call you when I am visual.'

Mmmm … I'm thinking, visual! It's filthy weather down there, sea state must be about 6 to 7, waves of 6-9 metres, 40 mph winds, low cloud and driving rain, not my idea of a living! But we did drop down to low-level earlier to identify the vessel, a fisherman onboard, injured when a cable hauling in his nets snapped! Yuk! That's why I am now sitting up here in my cosy Nimrod at 10,000 feet, warm and dry!

However, it is no sense of complacency up here, rather a feeling of admiration, not just for the crew of the approaching Sea King helicopter, scrambled some 3 hours ago out of Lossiemouth, but for all those individuals from the Rescue Services, both military and civilian, who are prepared to put their lives at risk to help, assist or even save the lives of others!

The crew will be commencing their on-scene checks now, the winchman preparing for the lowering down to the deck of a heaving, tossing fishing boat in the knowledge that if he fails and the fisherman doesn't get medical treatment soon, then all of their efforts could be for nowt! He will soon be cold, soaked and no doubt bruised from being thrown against the boat; his very life will depend on the skill of those in the helicopter above him and, of course, some good luck!

They are on their way home now, another successful 'lift' and, hopefully, another recovering individual. These people, men and women, are all real, everyday heroes, unsung and rarely seeking publicity, for that isn't the reason that they pursue their cause. My thoughts return to the warmth and comfort of my own environment, how I would love to share the same with them! In fact, a steaming bowl of Nimrod-renowned Honkers Stew would, I am certain, go down well! Hot (yes!) nutritious (well, fairly!) and filling (definitely!). Yes, that's what I would treat these REAL heroes to!

game & sausages

...diwala's Venison Sheek Kavaab • Pot Roast Venison • B
...sant with Root Vegetables • Spitfire Cassoulet • Bange
...umpy Pie • Rusi Todiwala's Venison Sheek Kavaab • Pot
• Braised Pheasant with Root Vegetables • Spitfire Cas
...s and Scrumpy Pie • Rusi Todiwala's Venison Sheek Ka
...t Venison • Braised Pheasant with Root Vegetables • S
... • Bangers and Scrumpy Pie • Rusi Todiwala's Venison
...Pot Roast Venison • Braised Pheasant with Root Vege
...pitfire Cassoulet • Bangers and Scrumpy Pie • Rusi Tod
...n Sheek Kavaab • Pot Roast Venison • Braised Pheas

My Hero

My Dad

I have often wondered who my hero is or even whether I have one. You always try to think of people who have amazed you, impressed you, people you wish to know or to meet but perhaps cannot, as they may be too distant, but our true heroes are often closer to home!

My food hero for sure is Chef Anton Mosimann, but my real hero is none other than Rustom Dhunjishaw Todiwala, my very own dad. Dad was from a rare breed of men who stood for all things right and fair and he had a deep understanding of the human mind that is seldom seen. He and Mum married rather late in life and he was fifty-one years old when I was born, not that anyone realised it because he was built like a rock and never looked a day older than thirty-five. Dad had amazing strength and was as fit as they come and it was this and his undiminished will-power and self-discipline that saw him to the ripe old age of ninety-seven, thereby allowing us the opportunity to marry and have our own children with him still present, affording us some fabulous memories.

He was a hugely talented man and was much gifted with his hands, and I am fortunate that I grew up around a man who could teach me so much, but above all else he taught me the value of life, of humanity, of feeling for my fellow beings and to be righteous, truthful, sincere and always honest; little do we realise as youngsters how much all this means. Today as I make my own progress and become recognised for some of my talents, much of what my father stood for and believed in comes to light and each time, I feel proud that my parents did what they did for me.

If I had one last chance to cook for him, it would definitely be Venison Sheek Kavaabs (kebabs, as they are better known in the UK). Dad was a great hunter and always told me that to get the best out of venison you must make kebabs as that way the meat is at its best, and I agree!

Rusi Todiwala's Venison Sheek Kavaab

Ingredients

500g venison shoulder meat
20g fresh coriander (including stalks)
20g fresh mint (including stalks)
2.5 cm-piece ginger
6–8 garlic cloves
1 fresh green chilli
1 tsp garam masala powder
1 tsp ground cumin
1 tsp ground coriander
½ tsp red chilli powder
½ tsp turmeric
1 tsp limejuice
salt

Method

1 Clean the meat well removing all the sinews and gristle. Do not discard any fat, if found.

2 Cut the meat into small pieces and mince all the ingredients together, except the powdered spices, salt and lime juice, which should be added to the mince, when finished. You can fry a small piece of the mince to check the salt. Then cover the mince and chill.

3 To cook the kebabs, either you need a tandoor or you can grill them over a BBQ. Get it very hot before you start forming the mince over the skewers.

4 Apply a little oil or water to the palm of your hand to prevent the mince sticking when moulding the kebabs. Form a ring between your forefinger and the thumb and use the rest of the fingers to guide the mince, applying pressure gently so that it thins itself out over the skewer, ideally about one inch in diameter. This does take a bit of practice!

5 Suspend each skewer on a small tray so that the minced area is suspended above it. When ready, cook them the same way over the BBQ, or insert in the tandoor as recommended by the manufacturer.

6 Don't overcook, as this makes the kebab dry and chewy. The kebab should ideally feel spongy, but should show signs of a liquid presence inside.

7 Serve with either fresh green chutney or onion salad and enjoy.

DIFFICULTY LEVEL	PREPARATION TIME	COOKING TIME	SERVES
MODERATE	15 MINUTES	5–10 MINUTES	4

Colonel Ian Blanks
Royal Engineer

My Hero
Sir Ranulph Fiennes OBE

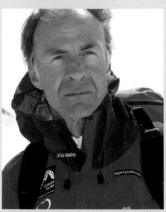

Sir Ranulph Fiennes has a fantastic ability to achieve goals despite seemingly insurmountable hurdles. A former soldier, he has an impressive list of achievements. Polar explorer, he and Charles Burton were the first to travel to both poles by land on the Transglobe Expedition in 1992. A marathon runner extraordinaire, seven marathons in seven continents in seven days; and a mountaineer, climbing the North Face of the Eiger and attempting Everest; all achieved despite suffering from cancer, heart problems and vertigo. To cap it all, through his adventures he has raised over five million pounds for charity. Sir Ranulph obviously has a penchant for the cold and polar regions and so I would feed him a typical Finnish dish – Reindeer Pot au Feu or Poronkeitto. (It works with venison too!)

As a soldier who has occasionally needed to find inspiration from elsewhere, and as a climber who has also looked down with trepidation at times, I find inspiration from Sir Ranulph's example.

180

Pot Roast Venison
Ingredients

500g venison bones
1 calf's foot
½ litre water
1 onion
1 tsp allspice
500g venison meat (shoulder)
2 carrots
1 celery stick
4 potatoes
25g pearl barley
1 leek
1 small bunch parsley

DIFFICULTY LEVEL	PREPARATION TIME	COOKING TIME	SERVES
MODERATE	30 MINUTES	2–3 HOURS APPROX	4

Method

1 Pre heat the oven to 200C / 400F / Gas Mark 6.

2 Put the venison bones and calf's foot into a roasting tin and roast for 30 minutes until lightly browned.

3 Move the venison bones and calf's foot from the roasting tin into a large saucepan.

4 Roughly chop the onion and add to the pan with the water and allspice. Bring to the boil, then reduce the heat and simmer for about 2 hours. Skim away any froth that appears.

5 Strain the stock into a clean pan. Add the venison meat and simmer gently for one hour and a half.

Pot Roast Venison

6 Cut the carrots, celery, leek and potatoes into large dice. Add the carrots and celery to the mixture and and simmer for 10 minutes. Add the potatoes and pearl barley and simmer for a further 10 minutes.

7 Finally add the leek and simmer, until the potatoes and barley are tender, add the chopped parsley and season.

8 To serve, slice into thick slices and serve in a bowl, with the vegetables and stock.

Major-General
Gerald Cavendish Grosvenor
The Duke of Westminster

My Hero
Alexander the Great

I have chosen Alexander the Great as the greatest of all great commanders: he stands head and shoulders above the rest. By the time of his death at thirty-three, he had led his armies through what was then a third of the known world, using tactics which had hitherto never been seen or experienced. He used flair and imagination with great flexibility. He was a leader in the true sense of the word, commanding as he did by instinct; he was the answer to the classic debate 'Is a leader born or made?' – he was a born leader.

Braised Pheasant with Root Vegetables and Redcurrant Jelly

Ingredients

2 dressed pheasants
8 slices pancetta or streaky bacon
1 large onion
4 cloves garlic
2 carrots
1 parsnip
½ swede
2 tbsp redcurrant jelly
½ bottle red wine
1 litre water
50g butter

Method

1 Remove the legs and breasts from the birds. Remove the skin from the breasts and wrap in the pancetta, then place in the fridge.

2 Cut the onion, carrots, parsnip and swede into small dice and finely crush the garlic.

3 In a pan, cook the remaining carcasses until they are golden in colour, then de-glaze with the red wine. Reduce the red wine down by half, then add the water and turn the heat down and simmer. Add the pheasant legs and cook them, until tender, 30–45 minutes.

4 When the legs are cooked (meat falling off the bone), shred the meat.

5 Place the meat to one side.

6 In another pan, brown the breasts in a little oil and place to one side, melt the butter and add the vegetables and saute until they are golden.

Braised Pheasant with Root Vegetables and Redcurrant Jelly

7 Add the redcurrant jelly and the shredded meat and place the breasts on top. Season and place in the oven for 6 minutes.

8 While the meat is in the oven, strain the cooking liquor from the other pan and thicken if required.

9 Serve the pheasant on top of the root vegetables and top with the sauce.

DIFFICULTY LEVEL	PREPARATION TIME	COOKING TIME	SERVES
DIFFICULT	30 MINUTES	1 HOUR APPROX	4

Squadron Leader Al Pinner MBE

Royal Air Force Squadron Leader. Officer Commanding the Battle of Britain Memorial Flight.

My Hero

Sir Douglas Bader

Being raised as the son of a post-war Meteor pilot, my bookshelves were crammed with all manner of wartime stories. While my father played a large part in my future choice of career, it was without doubt *Reach for the Sky*, the biography of Group Captain Sir Douglas Bader CBE DSO DFC, that inflamed my passion for flight.

To a young impressionable boy, his story was totally incredible: after losing his legs in a flying accident (through his own indiscipline) and missing out on potential England honours for rugby, he conquered the depths of despair and his physical disability and learnt to walk, drive and fly again, ending up the fifth most successful British fighter pilot in World War II with twenty-two and a half kills at the time he was shot down and taken prisoner.

Opinionated, dogmatic, forthright and at times insubordinate, he was also an incredibly charismatic wartime leader who led by example, showed no fear and gave no quarter. He was knighted in 1976 for his outstanding work for and amongst the disabled, and his legacy continues through the Douglas Bader Foundation and Flying Scholarships for the Disabled.

Were he to dine with me I would feed him a hearty Cassoulet, perfect for a cold winter's evening.

Spitfire Cassoulet

Ingredients

250g haricot beans
500g duck leg
500g venison sausage
(or any other sausage of your choice)
500g belly pork
1 large onion
2 cloves garlic
3 carrots
3 sprigs rosemary
3 sprigs sage
1 litre beef stock
½ litre red wine
1 tbsp flour

Method

1 Soak the haricot beans for at least 2 hours or, preferably, overnight.

2 Dice the duck, sausages and belly pork, removing some of the fat but not all, as this gives the flavour.

3 Peel and cut the onion into large cubes, peel and crush the garlic, then peel and dice the carrots.

4 Remove the sage from the sprigs.

5 Fry the diced meat in its own fat until brown, add onions and fry for a further 5 minutes.

6 Add the red wine and reduce by half, add the flour and stir in, add the stock gradually, until the flour is mixed in.

7 Add the carrots and herbs and cook slowly for 2–3 hours.

8 Remove sprigs of rosemary before serving.

DIFFICULTY LEVEL	PREPARATION TIME	COOKING TIME	SERVES
EASY	30 MINUTES	2–3 HOURS	4–6

My Hero
My Father

My father was a member of the Royal Ulster Constabulary (RUC) from 1946 and over the duration of the Troubles in Northern Ireland until his retirement in 1985. The severity and intensity of the Troubles meant that I saw little of my father at times; such was the nature of his job. My first awareness of what he actually did was seeing him on a live TV news flash where he and other members of the police and army were involved in an operation in West Belfast. The streets were lined with women and children, some banging bin lids off the ground and others throwing rocks, milk bottles and various other missiles at the authorities. At the same time I witnessed the terror and helplessness of my mother as we both watched the television. The whole experience, whilst a fairly minor one for my father, was an extremely distressing one for me. That day, I watched my dad being assaulted and in grave danger on national TV, and from then on he has been my hero.

Banger and Scrumpy Pie

Ingredients

6–8 potatoes
1 large onion
10–12 good pork sausages
1 small tin sweet corn
2 cooking apples
25g butter
200ml cider or gravy
50g cheese
1 packet crisps (optional)

Method

1 Pre heat the oven to 180C / 350F / Gas Mark 4.

2 Wash, peel and chop the potatoes and boil in a pan for 20–30 minutes, until soft enough to mash.

3 While the potatoes are boiling, grill the sausages until brown and cut into three.

4 Peel, chop and saute the onion.

5 Drain the sweet corn and add to a pie dish with the sausages and onions.

6 Peel and finely slice the apple and place on top of the sausages.

7 Add the gravy or cider.

8 Drain the potatoes, then mash them with the butter and pipe, or spread over the sausages.

9 Grate the cheese over the potatoes.

10 Put in the oven for 25 minutes. If using crisps, add in the last 10 minutes of cooking.

11 Serve with a portion of cooked mushrooms and a glass of cider.

Banger and Scrumpy Pie

DIFFICULTY LEVEL	PREPARATION TIME	COOKING TIME	SERVES
EASY	30 MINUTES	25 MINUTES	4

MS GILLIAN GEORGE

My partner is a serving member of the RAF and is part of a Squadron that regularly visits Iraq. I suppose I can only describe him being away as living on a rollercoaster: when he is in the most dangerous areas I am at the top of the rollercoaster – constantly fearing for him and dreading answering the phone! What's even worse is coming home to realize that I have missed a phone call from Iraq and not knowing if it was from him or about him.

I know that he is at the greatest risk of harm when he is on his way back to the main base and, to make it more difficult, during these trips there is always a ban on communications. This is when I head down the biggest dip of the rollercoaster ride, with twists and turns to shake you up and stir up the full range of emotions: fear, that sense of urgency that precedes the return, relief that he will soon be out of live fire danger, but also apprehension at the possibility of attacks en route and the knowledge that, although back at base, he is still not fully out of danger.

I am at the bottom of the rollercoaster and slightly more at ease when he is within the compound in a more reinforced and secured environment. Functioning day-to-day must go on, normal life has to take place. No one really sees that you can't sleep at night or that you cry when you watch the news; you carry on because you have to for your family. Even knowing that he is on his way home, the trip doesn't finish: Will he have changed? Will we have changed? How will we get back to the old routine? Will we still be able to function as a family? The journey doesn't really end until you watch him walk through the Arrival doors at the airport … that is until he starts packing his bags for his next trip.

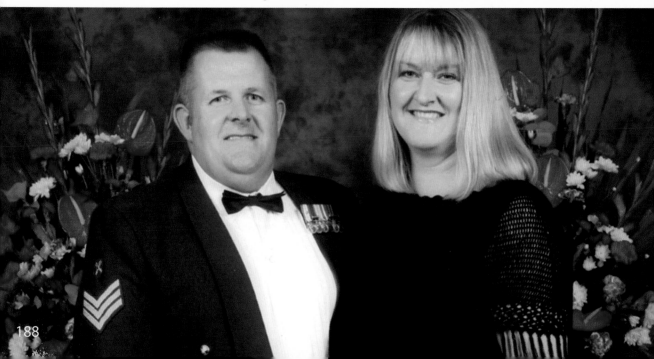

puddings & baking

Apple Crumble • Banoffi Pancakes • Spiced Plum and W
ble • Steamed Syrup Sponge • Sticky Toffee Stout Pud
berry Crumble • Hero Bear's Apple, Apricot and Hone
of Cornwall Light Infantry Pie • Thai Sticky Rice and M
son's Just Dessert • Boodle's Orange Fool • Vanilla-Cre
a • Fruit Salad with Chocolate Chip Ice Cream • Lemon
ry Conde • Raspberry Pavlova • Lovely Loaders' Loaf • V
e Brownies • Mum's Bakestones • Yummy Mummy's T
ney Buns • Apple Crumble • Banoffi Pancakes • Spiced
nut Crumble • Steamed Syrup Sponge • Sticky Toffee

Flight Lieutenant John Gorman
RAF Engineer

My Hero
Sir Frank Whittle

Anyone who knows me will be aware of my attraction to powerful cars. I've bored many with talk of horsepower, Newton metres, power ranges and the like. That was the reason I pushed myself in school and ended up doing an engineering degree, specialising in jet engines. The technology behind jet propulsion is fascinating, but the story behind the one man to whom it is credited is equally intriguing.

Despite his relative inexperience in the aerospace industry, Whittle never stopped pushing for technological improvement, and in 1938 he famously created the quantum leap in engine design: the turbojet. He ploughed so much of his own money into producing the engine that he did not have enough money left (£5 in those days) to patent his design. However, his efforts not only helped the Allies win the war, but he also boosted the British engineering industry, and created a technology that affects us all today in many ways: you wouldn't be flying abroad without the airliners that rely on jet engines to get them airborne.

Whittle was a strong character, which was just what we needed at that time in history; weaker men would have given

up long before. He was almost court-martialled for dangerous low-flying, and shortly after the jet engine's first test flight the pilot said to him, 'Frank, it flies.' Whittle replied, 'Well, that's what it was bloody well designed to do, wasn't it?'

The commitment that he showed should be an inspiration to all engineers today. I'd cook him the best recipe I know: Apple Crumble with custard. I salute Frank Whittle and marvel at his engineering triumph!

Apple Crumble
Ingredients

600g cooking apples
85g sugar
50ml water
170g self-raising flour
85g margarine
45g Demerara sugar

DIFFICULTY LEVEL	PREPARATION TIME	COOKING TIME	SERVES
EASY	20 MINUTES	20 MINUTES	4

Apple Crumble

Method

1 To make the apple base first peel and core the apples and then cut them into a small dice.

2 Put them into a saucepan with the water and sugar (more sugar can be added if needed to taste).

3 Cook the mix over a medium heat, stirring occasionally until the apples have softened.

4 Remove the mix from the heat and set aside for now.

5 For the crumble topping, rub the margarine into the flour until it resembles the consistency of breadcrumbs.

6 Add the sugar to the mix and stir in.

7 Place the cooked apple mix into the bottom of an ovenproof dish, cover evenly with the crumble mix and place into an oven, preheated to 200C / 400F / Gas Mark 6, for approximately 20 minutes, or until the top is golden brown and the mix bubbling.

8 Serve immediately with either a couple of scoops of ice cream or hot custard.

Air Chief Marshal Sir Glen Torpy
Chief of the Air Staff

My Hero
Lord Hugh Trenchard, Marshal of the RAF

As the Royal Air Force celebrates its 90th anniversary as the world's first independent Air Force it throws the spotlight on the individual who single-handedly, and with amazing foresight and determination, brought about this momentous change in military history – Lord Trenchard. Despite fierce resistance and scepticism from many quarters, Trenchard's vision, imagination, leadership and tenacity won through, and he can be justifiably proud of the profound effect he had on the conduct of modern military operations and the way he shaped the principles on which today's Royal Air Force is still founded. As such, he continues to inspire both young and old today, and has rightfully secured a place as my hero.

Spiced Plum and Walnut Crumble with Cinnamon Ice Cream

Ingredients

Ice cream:
4 medium egg yolks
100g castor sugar
1½ tsp ground cinnamon
1 vanilla pod
500ml double cream

Crumble:
12 plums
100g acacia honey
2 vanilla pods
1 orange
1 tsp mixed spice
100g plain flour
60g butter
50g castor sugar
100g walnuts
1 tsp ground nutmeg

Method

1 Halve one of the vanilla pods, scrape out the seeds and put in a thick-bottomed pan with the cream. Bring to the boil and leave to infuse for 10 minutes.

2 Whisk the egg yolks, sugar and cinnamon, strain on the cream and stir. Gently cook until the cream coats the back of a wooden spoon; don't let it boil. Strain and cool.

3 Put into an ice-cream machine or, in the freezer, turn the mixture by hand every 10 minutes.

Spiced Plum and Walnut Crumble with Cinnamon Ice Cream

DIFFICULTY LEVEL	PREPARATION TIME	COOKING TIME	SERVES
MODERATE	45 MINUTES	50 MINUTES	4

4 Split the plums, remove the stones and put, skins-side down, in a non-stick baking dish.

5 Scrape out the seeds from the other vanilla pod. Grate the orange zest. Mix together the honey, vanilla seeds, zest, orange juice and spices.

6 Pour this mixture over the plums and leave to marinade for 30 minutes. While plums are marinating, pre-heat oven to 150C / 300F / Gas Mark 2.

7 Roast plums for 15–20 minutes, until soft. When cool, turn upside down into the juices, cover with cling film and leave to cool completely.

8 Rub together the flour, butter, sugar and nutmeg until it resembles breadcrumbs, crush the walnuts and mix in.

9 Quarter the plums, cover with the crumble, bake at 170C / 325F /Gas Mark 3 for 20 minutes, until the crumble topping browns. Reserve the juices and use as extra sauce when serving.

Corporal Francesca Allen
RAF Chef

My Hero
Kate Ackril

My hero would have to be my mum, Kate Ackril. Corny I know, but it's the truth.

My mum has been through some unbelievably hard times in her life from losing her mum, my wonderful Nana, far too early, to going through the hardest time in her life when I was aged between five and sixteen (she knows what I mean). I have only ever seen my mum break down completely once, and when I think of all the things (I now realise with my grown-up eyes) she went through, this seems totally unbelievable to me.

I really hope I have inherited some of my mum's strength and resolve; however, I fear this is something from a different generation as I find myself phoning my mum on the slightest little thing. I think the last time I did this was when I wasn't feeling very well and popped into the supermarket for some milk and all I could smell the whole way round the shop was her perfume, which she has worn since I was a little girl. I instantly felt comforted, and found myself compelled to phone and tell her!

I myself can only hope my children (which I plan to have someday!) feel the same about me as I do about my wonderful, amazing mum, who I am very happy to say is a very happy and contented lady these days. Thank you, Mum, for everything you've done!

Because I am a chef I have cooked for my mum many times and obviously (!) she has always loved everything I've done for her, even the bright green, and I might add cold, pea soup I made her when I was about seven! My fear is she's just telling me what every mum tells her child … On this occasion I would cook her Traditional Steamed Syrup Sponge and Homemade Custard for two reasons: first, I know for a fact this is her favourite pudding, and second, I would love to be able to comfort my mum the way she has me every day from the day I was born, and I think this would make a pretty good start!

I really hope I have inherited some of my mum's strength and resolve . . .

Steamed Syrup Sponge and Homemade Custard

Ingredients

Sponge:
200g butter, at room temperature
200g caster sugar
1 tsp vanilla essence
200g plain flour
1 tsp baking powder
4 eggs
100g golden syrup

Custard:
350ml double cream
½ vanilla pods
6 egg yolks
100g caster sugar

DIFFICULTY LEVEL	PREPARATION TIME	COOKING TIME	SERVES
MODERATE	15 MINUTES	30–40 MINUTES	4

Method

1 Halve the vanilla pods, scrape out the seeds and put into a saucepan with the cream. Bring to just below boiling point over medium heat. Leave to cool and infuse.

2 Butter and flour four ramekins, and preheat the oven to 140C / 275F / Gas Mark 1. Beat or whisk the butter, sugar and vanilla essence together in a large bowl until no granules of sugar are left.

3 Sieve half the flour and baking powder into the butter mixture with two eggs, mix in slowly at first, then beat vigorously. Repeat with the remaining flour and eggs.

4 Microwave the syrup for 30 seconds so it pours easily and pour into the four ramekins, put the sponge mixture on top and cover tightly with cling film. Put the ramekins in a roasting dish and half fill it with boiling water, cling film the whole tin very tightly to seal and steam the sponges.

5 Bake in the oven for 30 minutes or so, they're ready when a skewer or tooth pick comes out clean from the centre of the sponge.

6 Meanwhile, whisk the egg yolks and sugar together, in a bowl over a hot pan of water, until thick and creamy.

7 Sieve the cream and mix a little with the egg mixture. Then put the mixture into the rest of the cream and stir thoroughly. Warm over a medium heat, stirring all the time, until it has thickened, don't allow it to boil!

8 Turn the sponges out into bowls and serve with the custard, which can be kept warm over a bain marie if necessary.

Tony Hadley
Frontman of 1980s legendary band Spandau Ballet

My Hero
Frank Sinatra

Simply one of the greatest singers in the world, Sinatra was a man who went through many highs and lows in his career and survived, which I really relate to. Despite what was written about him, one thing that sticks in my mind is whenever he played his concerts, all his wives and ex-girlfriends would be there together … so he can't have been all that bad, can he?! He was also an extremely generous man, who in his lifetime raised in excess of one billion dollars for charities across the world.

Sticky Toffee Stout Pudding
Ingredients

Pudding:
¾ bottle of Crazy Dog Stout (or similar)
200g ready to eat dates (ensure the stones are removed)
1 tsp vanilla extract
1 tsp instant coffee or an espresso
1 tsp bicarbonate soda
5–6 tbsp Demerara sugar
110g soft butter, plus extra for greasing
175g molasses sugar
3 large eggs
225g self-raising flour

Sauce:
the remaining stout
200g molasses sugar
75g butter
200ml whipping cream

Method

1 Preheat the oven to 190C / 375F / Gas Mark 5 (fan oven – 175C / 325F / Gas Mark 3).

2 Place the dates in a bowl with the vanilla and coffee.

3 Heat the stout and pour over the date mixture and stir in the bicarbonate of soda.

4 Leave to cool completely.

5 When chilled, blend in a food processor until almost smooth, set aside.

6 Thoroughly line your pudding basins with butter and sprinkle liberally with some of the molasses sugar.

7 Cream the remaining dark brown sugar and butter until fluffy.

Sticky Toffee Stout Pudding

8 Add the eggs and combine the flour. Don't worry if the mixture looks a little curdled.

9 Lastly, add the date puree and whisk (this can be done by hand).

10 Spoon the mixture into the basins and bake in the centre of the oven, until you can insert a skewer and it comes out clean. This will take about 25 minutes.

11 Remove from the oven and set aside.

12 To make the sauce, place all ingredients in a heavy bottom pan and bring to a gentle boil until all the sugar has dissolved.

13 If you like a thicker toffee sauce, thicken with a little corn flour.

14 Turn the puddings out and slice, from the bottom up, three or four slices.

15 Layer back into basins with the sticky toffee stout sauce, ensuring all the pudding is covered, including the tops.

16 Grill for a couple of minutes until crunchy.

17 Serve with loads and loads of chilled fresh cream or ice cream.

These little puds can be made up to a couple of days in advance and reheated at the same temperature for 15–20 minutes or, in a microwave, for 40–50 seconds.

DIFFICULTY LEVEL	PREPARATION TIME	COOKING TIME	SERVES
MODERATE	30–40 MINUTES	25 MINUTES	8

Fern Britton
TV Presenter

My Hero

All our injured heroes, and the remarkable people who help them get their lives back on track

My heroes are the people this book will help. The media is painfully full of stories of servicemen and women who have paid the ultimate sacrifice in service of their country and in the name of freedom. Nothing should be taken away from their sacrifice, and of course our hearts go out to those who will not see their loved ones return: they too are heroes. But we must not forget those who have returned, who need support to get their lives back on track. The tales of bravery and dignity of the many individuals who are scarred by operations are heart wrenching. It is about returning the most fundamental human freedoms to those individuals: the ability to walk, see and hear. This involves the efforts of exceptional people who often have to deal with the most harrowing of circumstances, albeit to a rewarding end. These men have displayed exceptional courage and determination in their fight to adapt to a new way of life; and the dedicated, hard-working specialists at Headley Court and all other military medical establishments deserve all of our support and gratitude for their efforts. To say thank you to my hero I would cook a roast lamb with all the trimmings – followed up with a gooseberry crumble.

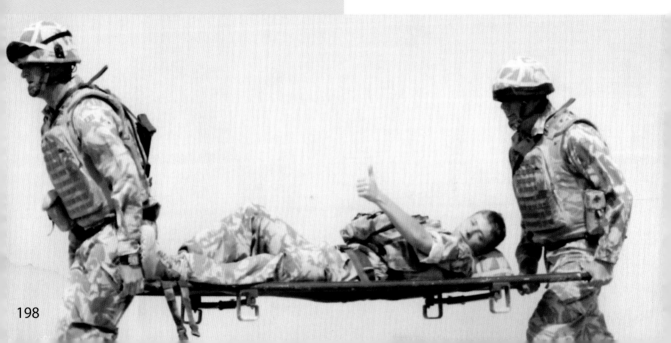

Gooseberry Crumble

Ingredients

200g flour
100g butter
100g oats
100g caster sugar
3x425g tins gooseberries
100g custard powder
125g icing sugar
50g soft brown sugar

Method

For the roast lamb dinner please see recipe on page 119.

1 To make the crumble topping put the flour in a large mixing bowl and cut the butter into cubes. Using your fingertips, rub the butter into the flour until the mix becomes a sandy, breadcrumb consistency.

2 Fold in the caster sugar and oats.

3 Next drain the gooseberries, gently fold the custard powder and icing sugar into them, and put them all in the bottom of a large ovenproof dish. Put the crumble on top of the gooseberries and sprinkle with the brown sugar.

4 Bake in a preheated oven at 180C / 350F / Gas Mark 4 for about 30-40 minutes until the top is crispy and golden brown.

5 Serve with custard, cream or ice cream.

DIFFICULTY LEVEL	PREPARATION TIME	COOKING TIME	SERVES
EASY	20 MINUTES	30–40 MINUTES	8–10

Hero Bear
The Mascot of Help for Heroes

My Hero
Winnie the Pooh

I am delighted to say that I have eaten this book from cover to cover and can recommend every recipe. It was not easy and sacrifices had to be made, not least to my waistline, but I have now done my duty and can return to hibernation with a sense of satisfaction and a full tummy.

As to choosing a hero, it is such a difficult one as there have been so many famous bears. I could have included Rupert but find his trousers a little loud, Pudsey would be good as he has clearly been hurt and would identify with the soldiers, Paddington is a favourite, but I have to settle for my personal hero ... Pooh!

Pooh is everything a bear should be: thoughtful, curious and motivated by an endless appetite for honey;
I am sure he would like this pie.

Hero Bear's Apple, Apricot and Honey Pie
Ingredients

6 large Bramley apples
250g bag dried apricots
250ml orange juice
3 tbsp honey
200g plain flour
100g butter
250ml water
sugar to sprinkle
milk to wash over
oil to grease plate

Hero Bear's Apple, Apricot and Honey Pie

Method

1 Preheat oven to 180C / 360F / Gas Mark 5.

2 Peel and chop the apples.

3 Cut the apricots in half and poach in orange juice for about 5 minutes until soft.

4 Drain the apricots and cook in a saucepan with the apples for 5–10 minutes until soft.

5 Add honey and leave to cool.

6 Mix butter to sieved flour and rub, until it resembles breadcrumbs.

7 Add water gradually, until mixture comes together.

8 Cut pastry in half. Roll one half to the size of a ceramic or aluminium plate, suitable for oven use.

9 Oil the plate and lay the pastry over it.

10 When cool, add apple mixture.

11 Roll out the other half of the pastry and top the pie.

12 Wash with milk, then sprinkle with sugar.

13 Cook for 25–30min.

14 Good served with custard, cream or ice cream.

DIFFICULTY LEVEL	PREPARATION TIME	COOKING TIME	SERVES
MODERATE	30 MINUTES	25–30 MINUTES	6

Lance Corporal Nick Gillan
Army Chef

My Hero
Ross Kemp

I met Ross Kemp while I was in Afghanistan and he immediately struck me as a bloke who not only understood what makes us tick, but also as someone who gets us and our sense of humour; that ability to have a dangerous experience one minute and to be able to laugh it off with the boys 20 minutes later. His TV show, Kemp in Afghanistan, is different from the majority of the documentaries that come out of theatre in that he puts himself on-the-line alongside the troops to show how it really is; even when he is clearly scared stupid, he doesn't try to hide it. A lot of us like to watch the show because it isn't a dressed-up over-blown drama designed to impress people sitting in their front rooms; what you see is what we get. In my opinion he took up the wrong profession, he would have made a great soldier.

courtesy of The Sun/NI Syndication

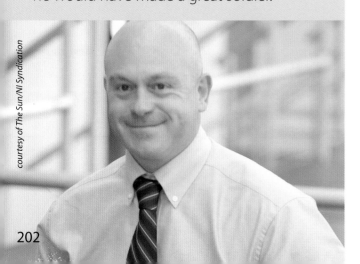

Banoffi Pancakes
Ingredients

For the filling:
1 tin condensed milk
5 bananas
cream

For the pancake batter:
110g plain flour
2 eggs
200ml milk
75ml water
vegetable oil and butter

Method

1 Cover the condensed milk tin (don't open or pierce it) with water, and bring to the boil, cover the pan and simmer for 2 hours, topping up with water as needed.

2 Sift the flour into a large bowl, add the eggs and mix to create a thick mixture. Mix the milk and water together and stir in gradually, then whisk rapidly to a thin, smooth batter. Sieve out any small lumps.

3 Heat a little oil in a frying pan until very hot. Turn the heat down a little and, using a pastry brush, smear a little butter onto the pan. Carefully ladle the batter into the pan, spreading it thinly by tilting the pan from side to side.

4 Keep the pan hot between pancakes, brushing on a little butter before each one. Separate cooked pancakes with greaseproof paper.

Banoffi Pancakes

5 Run the cold tap over the tin for 5 minutes, to cool it enough for handling. Open it carefully and spoon the toffee mixture into a pan, adding cream to make a thick sauce consistency. Put on the heat with the sliced bananas to warm through.

6 Heat the pancakes through at around 150C / 300F / Gas Mark 2, for 5–10 minutes.

7 Put the mixture in the pancakes and fold over, serve with a dusting of icing sugar.

DIFFICULTY LEVEL	PREPARATION TIME	COOKING TIME	SERVES
MODERATE	30 MINUTES	* 2 HOURS PLUS 20 MINUTES	6–8 PANCAKES

2 hours for the toffee and an extra 20 minutes for the pancakes

LANCE CORPORAL
NICK GILLAN

Nick Gillan is a Service Chef who spent the summer of 2008 working at a Forward Operating Base (FOB) in Afghanistan with the function of keeping fed anything up to 150 servicemen and women.

We'd been in the FOB for 4 weeks and had been receiving food drops via C-130 Hercules airdrops at irregular timeslots. The different types of food received were not ideal but when they were being dropped from 300ft at 100mph you can't really be too picky. We were usually given three-quarters Operational Ration Packs (ORP) and one quarter fresh food, including milk, eggs, flour, rice, sausages, bacon and oil, etc. Any chef worth his salt (no pun intended) can produce really good nutritional menus when these basics are used well with the ORPs.

On one memorable occasion, we were starting to run extremely low on rations but we weren't really worried due to the fact that we were expecting a ration drop that night. However, what should have been a routine drop of both a material re-supply and our precious rations turned out to be anything but. We could see the C-130 flying by, dropping the crates out of the back as usual. The first eight crates came down as planned, dropping a short distance out of the back of the aircraft before

the parachutes deployed and they began their slow, safe descent to earth. The next four (which unfortunately just happened to contain the food) left the aircraft and plummeted to the ground, landing with an almighty thump and a cloud of dust, throwing fresh and tinned food alike in every direction.

Now although it was still morning, it gets very hot very early in July in the middle of the desert, and by the time we attempted to recover what we could, this smashed assortment of food had been cooking away merrily for quite some time. Believe me, rummaging through 14 days worth of smashed rations in full body armour in hostile territory is anything but fun. The raw meat, ketchup, eggs, flour and all of the rest of the smashed food created an extremely unpleasant stinking sloppy mess. However, the thought of 150 hungry soldiers seriously focuses the mind and we recovered what we could. A little ingenuity and the best use of the tinned rations we still had got us through the fortnight.

... by the time we attempted to recover what we could, this smashed assortment of food had been cooking away merrily for quite some time.

Everyone ate well and needless to say all eyes were on the next drops which thankfully went to plan and contained a very welcome supply of decent fresh foods.

A 10-man Operational Ration Pack

A 10-man Operational Ration Pack is a food hamper given to military chefs working out of field kitchens. It is like having a larder in the box that chefs can use in the desert to create three meals for 10 servicemen and women.

Much of the food inside is canned, pre-cooked, freeze-dried, powdered or concentrated so that the chefs can quickly prepare food for troops on the battlefield.

Each box contains a variety of long-life rations, with high-calorie and high-energy content. A typical hamper includes food like tinned vegetables and fruit, dried yeast and herbs, flour, dried eggs, tinned meat, packets of dried sauces and custard powder, pasta, dried onions and bags of rice.

Using the contents of a 10-man ration pack, field chefs are able to prepare everything from fresh bread and a full English breakfast to balti curries, stir-fry dishes and even souffles. There are currently five different hampers available.

To help the chefs get the most out of their ration packs Defence Food Services have created a recipe book, with support from Gordon Ramsay.

My Hero

Field Marshal The Viscount Slim KG GCB GCMG GCVO GBE DSO MC

My hero is Field Marshal The Viscount Slim KG GCB GCMG GCVO GBE DSO MC of XIVth Army fame from Burma in WWII. He was described by Admiral of the Fleet Earl Mountbatten, the Supreme Allied Commander of Southeast Asia, as 'the finest general World War II produced'. His book Defeat into Victory is an amazing insight, master class of command and gripping account of the war in the Far East and in particular how the XIVth Army, under Slim's leadership, turned around a perilous situation and brought about a crushing defeat of the Japanese in Burma. The man is a truly inspirational leader.

General Sir William Slim (D 25026) by permission of the Imperial War Museum

Thai Sticky Rice and Mango (Khao Nieow Ma Muang)

Ingredients

320g raw sweet or glutinous rice (use Thai sticky rice if possible)

100g coconut milk for mixing in the rice (do not shake the can before opening; use the thick part that's usually on top).

60g sugar

½ tbsp salt for mixing in the rice

¼ tsp rice flour

100g very thick coconut milk for topping the rice

1/8 tsp salt for the topping

2 medium, ripe mangos

Method

1 Peel and slice the mangos, set aside.

2 Wash and rinse the rice well, add water to the rice to cover and come about a quarter of an inch off the surface. Cook the rice very slowly, bring to the boil and simmer for 2 minutes then turn the heat off, cover and leave for 45 minutes, do not stir.

3 Heat the first batch of coconut milk slowly in a saucepan. Add the sugar and half a tablespoon of salt and cook until the sugar has dissolved. Pour over the cooked rice, stir well and stand for around 30 minutes.

4 Heat the rest of the coconut milk and rice flour and add the salt, stir until the salt has dissolved, this makes the topping sauce.

5 Serve the sticky rice on a plate, garnish with mangos and top the rice with some of the sauce.

Thai Sticky Rice and Mango (Khao Nieow Ma Muang)

DIFFICULTY LEVEL	PREPARATION TIME	COOKING TIME	SERVES
FAIRLY EASY	20 MINUTES	1½ HOUR	4

My Hero
Guy Gibson

There can be few characters from the Second World War who better epitomise the spirit, courage and character of the bomber crews than Wing Commander Guy Gibson VC. At the age of twenty-four, he led the crews of 617 Squadron against the German dams in 1943 and delivered the famous Barnes Wallis 'bouncing bomb' at night whilst flying at sixty feet above the lakes, and being shot at. After he released his bomb he remained in the target area, drawing enemy fire and allowing the following aircraft as free a run as possible to the dam. The Dams Raids combined the ingenuity of Wallis with the raw courage of Gibson and serve as an inspirational example to all those who serve today. The debate on the effectiveness of the Raids continues to this date, but what is beyond doubt is that Gibson demonstrated leadership, determination and valour of the highest order. Wallis described Gibson as, 'A man born for war ... but born to fall in war', which sadly he did in 1944.

Gibson's Just Dessert

Ingredients

500ml heavy cream
1 tsp vanilla extract
6 egg yolks
10 tbsp caster sugar

Method

1 Pre-heat the oven to 120C / 260F / Gas Mark 1.

2 Put the cream in a saucepan with the vanilla and put over a low heat, slowly bring to just before boiling point and then turn off the heat and leave for 20 minutes. This enhances the flavour of the vanilla.

3 Meanwhile, put the egg yolks in a large bowl and whisk with 4 tablespoons of the sugar (reserving the rest for the caramelized tops). Whisk the mix until the sugar has dissolved and the mixture is thick, pale and yellow.

4 Pour a little of the warm cream into the yolk mix and stir in, now pour the yolk mix into the cream and whisk to incorporate, put the pan back onto a low heat and, stirring all the time. Wait until the mix has thickened and coats the back of a spoon.

5 Divide the mix among 6 ramekins or custard cups. Put the ramekins in a water bath (large, deep ovenproof container filled with 1-2 inches boiling water) and bake in the oven until set around the edges but still loose in the centre, around 50 minutes to an hour.

6 Remove from the oven and keep the ramekins in the water bath, until the mix has cooled, put the ramekins in the fridge and chill for 2 hours (but overnight is better).

Gibson's Just Dessert

7 When ready to serve, sprinkle 2 teaspoons of the remaining sugar over each custard.

8 For best results use a small kitchen blowtorch to melt the sugar until golden brown and bubbling. If you don't have a blowtorch, put them under a very hot grill until the same happens. Rechill the custards for 20 minutes before serving.

DIFFICULTY LEVEL	PREPARATION TIME	COOKING TIME	SERVES
EASY	15 MINUTES	1 HOUR	3

My Hero
John Charles

My hero is a footballer, not because he played for my team Leeds United and not because he was the first British player to make the grade in Italian football, but because he was rightly christened by the fans of Juventus as 'Il Buon Gigante' – the gentle giant.

This man was a true sportsman and one who many could take as a role model when competing in any sport.

He was a world-class centre half and centre forward and one of the most versatile footballers ever, playing full back and mid field when needed. Indeed he broke the Leeds United scoring record with forty-two goals in a season whilst playing International football at centre half.

John Charles was instrumental in taking Leeds United from the second division to the top flight in English football and was also a greatly respected footballer in Italy. In his latter years he became a friend of my father who always spoke of him with such admiration. This was a man of whom the great Danny Blanchflower said, 'My feet do not do my thinking for me as they do for John Charles, that's why I can never be as great a footballer as he.'

But for me he will always remain the 'gentle giant', a man never cautioned, never sent off, but still a winner, and that is what sport is all about.

My recipe for John Charles would salute a great man and would take us an age to eat so we could spend time talking. Sadly John Charles has passed away.

courtesy of The Sun/NI Syndication

Boodle's Orange Fool
Ingredients

12 sponge rings to fit into Martini glasses
50g marmalade
4 oranges
2 lemons
200g caster sugar
2 oranges
500ml double cream

DIFFICULTY LEVEL	PREPARATION TIME	COOKING TIME	SERVES
EASY	20 MINUTES	0	6

Boodle's Orange Fool

Method

1 Sandwich 2 discs of sponge cake with marmalade.

2 Grate the rind from the orange and lemon and squeeze the juice.

3 Add the sugar to the juice and mix thoroughly.

4 Segment the other 2 oranges.

5 Put the segmented oranges into the glasses and top with the sponge.

6 Whip three-quarters of the cream until thick but not stiff.

7 Slowly beat the juices into the cream.

8 Spoon over the cake and chill the cream until it sets and the juice has separated over the cake, preferably overnight.

9 Whip the rest of the cream and pipe on top, decorate with either orange rind or chocolate, the choice is yours.

My Hero

Sir Bobby Charlton

My personal hero from my childhood has to be Sir Bobby Charlton because he was everybody's football icon and a perfect professional and gentleman, which is sometimes lacking in today's society.

There is a correlation between what we do in the hospitality industry and what Bobby Charlton achieved in his field in the fact that he realised it is about performing to the best of your ability; he gave 100% each time he went on to the field. Sir Bobby's aim was to provide value for money for his audiences and this inspired me to have the same outlook in life in ensuring our guests return for more of the same standards. In much the same way that Sir Bobby connected with the supporters he played in front of, we have to connect with our guests who pay good money to be entertained. In my opinion, Sir Bobby certainly achieved all of these goals in his career and will probably be one of very few to do so.

Vanilla-Creamed Tapioca
with Armagnac-Poached Prunes with Hazelnut Crunch Crumble

Ingredients

Tapioca:
100g tapioca
400g milk
25g sugar
1 vanilla pod
100g cream

Prunes:
110g water
50g sugar
70g Armagnac
120g stoned prunes

Hazelnut crunch:
50g flaked hazelnuts
100g ground hazelnuts
100g flour
70g butter
50g sugar

Method

1 Put the tapioca into cold water and bring to the boil. Cook for a few minutes until the starch starts to thicken the water, then put into a strainer and run under cold water.

2 Repeat this process except this time don't run under cold water.

3 Bring the milk, sugar and vanilla pod to the boil.

4 Turn down to a simmer and add the tapioca.

5 Once it is cooked sufficiently, take off the heat and add the cream.

6 Allow to cool and adjust the consistency with milk, if necessary.

7 For the prunes, bring the stock syrup and Armagnac to the boil.

8 Add the prunes and cook till soft. Cool.

Vanilla-Creamed Tapioca
with Armagnac-Poached Prunes with Hazelnut Crunch Crumble

DIFFICULTY LEVEL	PREPARATION TIME	COOKING TIME	SERVES
MODERATE	20 MINUTES	30 MINUTES	4

9 To make the crumble, toast the flaked nuts, and then mix the rest of the ingredients to make the crumble.

10 Bake in the oven at 165C / 325F / Gas Mark 3 for about 10–15 minutes, until golden brown.

11 To serve, arrange the bottom of the dish with prunes. Put tapioca on top, then a whole poached prune in the centre and sprinkle the outer rim of the bowl with crushed crumble mixture.

Ross Kemp
Actor and Presenter

courtesy of The Sun/NI Syndication

My Hero
The British Armed Forces

I first went to Afghanistan to learn about the lives of ordinary soldiers and to try to understand the pressures they are under in one of the most dangerous places in the world today.

It was a pretty humbling experience and it was a privilege to witness their courage, tenacity and professionalism.

If we expect our young men and women to put their lives on the line for us, they should be paid accordingly, have the correct equipment and should be given proper healthy food.

Napoleon once said that 'an army marches on its stomach'. In order for our boys and girls to keep themselves healthy they need, and the one thing that I missed whilst I was on the ground, is healthy green stuff. Therefore my suggestion, particularly during the hot months, would be for them to have Mediterranean salad followed by a fruit salad.

Fresh Fruit Salad with Chocolate Chip Ice Cream

Ingredients

Ice Cream:
10 chocolate chip cookies
2 vanilla pods
3 litres cream
500g sugar
2 egg yolks

Fruit Salad:
1 pear
1 red apple
1 green apple
225g redcurrants
225g strawberries
1 kiwi fruit
1litre orange juice

Method

1 Crush down the cookies to a crumb consistency and then take the seeds from the vanilla pod.

2 Place the cream and vanilla pods in a thick-bottomed pan and bring to the boil, then switch off, leaving to infuse for 10 minutes.

3 Whisk egg yolks and sugar until it doubles in size and is pale in colour.

4 Strain cream mixture onto the yolks and stir well. Pour into a clean saucepan and place back onto the stove.

5 Stirring with a wooden spoon, gently cook until the cream coats the back of a spoon, do not allow the mixture to boil, as it will split.

6 Strain into a clean container and allow to cool. When cool, add the cookie crumbs.

7 Churn in an ice-cream machine or, in the freezer, turning the mix by hand every 15 minutes until firm.

8 For the fresh fruit salad, wash and cut up all the fruit to your desired size.

9 Add orange juice and serve with the cookie ice cream. It's a lovely light meal.

Fresh Fruit Salad with Chocolate Chip Ice Cream

DIFFICULTY LEVEL	PREPARATION TIME	COOKING TIME	SERVES
EASY	30–45 MINUTES	0	4 APPROX

My Hero
Daley Thompson

Daley Thompson was probably the greatest ever decathlete in the history of athletics and was a real inspiration to me when I was starting out. I originally trained as a decathlete so I fully understood the raw talent and commitment it took for him to achieve his 4 world records and 2 Olympic records, as well as winning his World, Commonwealth and European titles.

Lemon Tart
Ingredients

Pastry:
250g flour
100g icing sugar
100g butter
2 eggs

Filling:
150ml double cream
100g caster sugar
4 eggs
3 lemons
12 tbsp lemon juice
icing sugar

Method

1 Preheat the oven to 190C / 375F / Gas Mark 5.

2 First, make the pastry: put the flour, sugar and butter into a bowl and rub together until it resembles breadcrumbs.

3 Add the eggs and mix until a soft mix has formed. Place cling film over the top and put into the fridge for 30 minutes.

4 Roll out the pastry on a floured surface and line either a 24cm quiche tin or individual quiche tins. Prick with a fork.

5 Line the tin with blind bake (lentils or rice on top of baking or greaseproof paper cut to the size of the pie) this will stop the pastry bubbling.

6 Bake for 15 minutes. Remove the blind bake.

7 For the filling, grate the rind off the three lemons and squeeze the juice, whisk the cream, eggs, sugar, lemon juice and rind.

8 Pour the mix into tin and bake for a further 20 minutes until just set.

9 Dust with icing sugar just before you serve.

Lemon Tart

DIFFICULTY LEVEL	PREPARATION TIME	COOKING TIME	SERVES
MODERATE	30 MINUTES	35 MINUTES	8

My Hero

The nameless mine victim of Cambodia.

North West Cambodia November 1993

Every few weeks I went to the hospital to interview the new mine casualties. He was lying on a metal bed with a reed mat covering the bed springs. His wife fanned his thin fever ravished body. As I walked towards him Fernanda the Spanish nurse smiled, shook her head and gestured to the next patient. I walked past him making eye contact trying to convey kindness and comfort when suddenly he grabbed my hand like a drowning man grasping something that floats and kept repeating 'How will I feed my children?'

He was covered with blasted gravel injuries and flash burns. Both his legs had been amputated and his children of two and four sat where his legs should have been. I replied that first he had to make himself believe he would live, then I knew a charity who would teach him to be a woodcarver so he could earn a living. After what seemed an eternity he nodded and let go of my hand. I told the charity about him and knew he'd be okay.

During the year it took him to learn to be a woodcarver he was given money to buy food. He saved it and ate the food everyone else threw away. Within a year he'd saved enough to buy some land and start building a house for his family. He worked so hard at woodcarving he became a teacher and he inspired me to run my first marathon within a year of leaving hospital to raise money for a new teaching building. I chose him as my hero because in the circumstances he was in, it's easier to give up and die. He fought for life and then took responsibility all the way for himself and his family, he bravely took the pain and got on with it.

The dinner I'd cook for him would start with Amok (a fish soup in coconut milk and spices), followed by sour chicken soup with lemon grass and for desert a cold creamy rice pudding with strawberry sauce; all washed down with a moderate amount of cava as I wouldn't want him to get any more legless than he is already.

Strawberry Conde

Ingredients

75g short grain rice (long grain rice works as well)
650ml milk
50g sugar
1 lemon
300ml evaporated milk
200g strawberries (or any berries of your choice)
3 tbsp sugar
3–4 tbsp water

DIFFICULTY LEVEL	PREPARATION TIME	COOKING TIME	SERVES
FAIRLY EASY	10 MINUTES	30–45 MINUTES	2

Method

1 First peel a twist of rind from the lemon with a knife (so it can be extracted), then put the rice milk, lemon rind and sugar into a saucepan and bring to the boil, simmer until soft and creamy, approximately 30–45 minutes, stirring regularly.

2 Let it cool, then fold in the evaporated milk.

3 For the fruit, put the fruit water and sugar into a pan and cook, when it's a glook, rather than a sauce or compote, it's ready (smells right), then leave to cool.

4 When cool, put fruit at the bottom of a glass, add the rice, decorate with fruit and enjoy.

My Hero

Jimmy James

The RAF produced many heroes during World War II, but in my mind there is no doubt that Jimmy James, for his determination and courage over a long period of time, is one of the greatest.

He took part in the 'Great Escape' from Stalag Luft 3, Sagan, and was captured after several weeks. Jimmy was fortunate enough not to be amongst the fifty fellow escapees murdered by the Gestapo; however, he was taken to Sachsenhausen, a death camp, but despite spending months in solitary confinement, he managed to tunnel his way out. In all, Jimmy made thirteen attempts to escape, for which he was awarded the Military Cross. His funeral was meant to be a private one, but Ludlow Church was full. Ludlow was his hometown and practically all the inhabitants lined the streets to say farewell. The RAF provided a Guard of Honour, and four Tornados from his former squadron flew over in a 'missing man' formation. A Canadian fellow-prisoner telephoned me to say that a number of them had watched it on the Internet and thought it was a state funeral.

Jimmy was a modest and unassuming gentleman but, to me, he was one of the RAF's greatest ever heroes.

Raspberry Pavlova and Cream

Ingredients

4 eggs
250g caster sugar
½ tsp cornflour
½ tsp white wine vinegar
½ tsp boiling water
200ml cream

Method

1 Preheat the oven to 120C / 250F / Gas Mark 1.

2 Separate the eggs, making sure there is no yolk in the whites.

3 Whisk the whites until the mixture forms stiff peaks. Add the sugar gradually and keep whisking. Ensure all equipment used is clean and free from grease.

4 Add the corn flour, white wine vinegar and the boiling water.

5 Pipe mix onto either greaseproof paper or sugar paper or non-stick mats. Either one large one or individual nests.

6 Cook for 1–1½ hours until pale in colour but firm to the touch.

7 Leave to dry out.

8 Whisk the cream until the mixture forms peaks.

9 Pipe onto meringue, dress with the raspberries and garnish with mint.

This can also be finished with any other berries of your choice.

Raspberry Pavlova and Cream

Lady Alison Loader
Wife of Commander-In-Chief Air Command

My Hero
The families left behind

Very hard to choose one hero – all the people in the armed forces are heroes really – but I have chosen the wives and husbands left behind to make my banana loaf for – they keep the children happy and the home life ticking along when the men and women are away. I know how hard that can be!

Lovely Loaders' Loaf!
(Banana and Walnut Loaf)

Ingredients

75g soft margarine or extra soft butter
(plus extra for greasing)
100g caster sugar
1 large egg (beaten)
225g plain flour
2 level tsp baking powder
4 medium ripe bananas
50g walnuts
grated zest of 1 lemon and 1 orange

Method

1 Preheat the oven to 180C / 350F / Gas Mark 4.

2 Grease a 3½ x 7½ inch loaf tin and line with greaseproof paper.

3 Put margarine or butter in a bowl with the sugar and egg; sift in the flour and baking powder. Mix until thoroughly combined (this may look a little dry).

4 Peel and mash the bananas with a fork so there are no large lumps of banana left, add to the mix, roughly chop the walnuts and add them along with the orange and lemon zest, mix thoroughly.

5 Put the mix into the prepared tin and level off.

6 Put in the oven on the centre shelf for 50 minutes to an hour, until well risen and springy, (it is also a good idea to test the cake with a knife, it should come out clean).

7 Leave to cool in the tin for 5 minutes, then loosen around the edges and cool on a wire tray.

This is really delicious spread with butter and is great to take on picnics with the children.

Lovely Loaders' Loaf!
(Banana and Walnut Loaf)

DIFFICULTY LEVEL	PREPARATION TIME	COOKING TIME	SERVES
EASY	15 MINUTES	1 HOUR	8–10

Lieutenant Jim Berry

1st Battalion, The Royal Irish Regiment

My Hero
Fred Berry

'I was injured while serving with '3 Para' on Operation HERRICK 4. I've had a bit of a think about what a hero is to me since being hurt. Celebrities aren't 'heroes'; they are just someone famous. To me, a hero is an ordinary person.

My grandfather fought through the Second World War, serving with the Royal Marines on HMS *King George V* during the hunt for – and subsequent sinking of – the Bismark; and in Africa, Sicily and mainland Italy, France and Germany to name a few. He was the only man from his troop to survive the Normandy Landings. He then continued to serve, serving on HMS *Belfast* during the Yangtze River Incident to rescue the stricken HMS *Amethyst*, and in Hong Kong and the Far East. He never thought anything of having done all these things, and rarely spoke of them.

What would I serve him? Just what he would ask for – bakestones, or Welsh cakes as you might know them. I'd make him a cup of tea to go with them, or pour him a pint – depending on whether he was sat in his favourite chair watching the cricket or if he was out in the garden watching the birds with his binoculars.

Mum's Bakestones

Ingredients

200g self-raising-flour
100g hard margarine
150g caster sugar
½ tsp mixed spice
1 small egg
150g mixed fruit

Method

1 Rub flour, margarine, sugar and mixed spice until the mixture resembles breadcrumbs.

2 Beat the egg, then add the breadcrumb mix until dough comes together. If the mix is too dry, add a little milk.

3 Knead in the mixed fruit.

4 Roll out until it is about a quarter of an inch thick, the size of cutter depends on how big you would like them.

5 Put a 'bake stone' or thick-bottomed pan onto the stove with a medium heat.

6 To check if it is hot enough, sprinkle on a little flour and it should brown within seconds.

7 Do not grease the pan. Lay the cakes around the outside and cook on either side for 3–4 minutes.

8 Serve with a nice cup of tea.

DIFFICULTY LEVEL	PREPARATION TIME	COOKING TIME	SERVES
MODERATE	20 MINUTES	25–30 MINUTES	24 CAKES

Mum's Bakestones

Corporal Hannah Simson
RAF Administrator

My Hero
Sir David Attenborough

Sir David is my hero for promoting environmental causes through his work. He has spent over fifty years tirelessly trekking to every corner of the world filming amazing sights. He has helped people to see all sorts of places and animals from all over the planet that they wouldn't dream of seeing otherwise. Most importantly he has helped us understand the impact human activity is having on the environment.

Vanilla Chocolate Brownies

Ingredients

300g Belgian dark chocolate
190g salted butter
5 eggs
340g golden caster sugar
1 vanilla pods seeds
225g plain flour
1 tsp baking powder
70g chopped walnuts

Method

1 Preheat the oven to 180C / 350F / Gas Mark 4.

2 Line a 20x30 cm baking tin with greaseproof paper.

3 Melt the chocolate and butter in a double boiler (heat proof bowl over a simmering saucepan of water).

4 Beat the eggs and sugar together, adding in the vanilla pod seeds.

5 Add the cooled chocolate mixture into the eggs and sugar.

6 Gradually fold into the mixture the sifted flour and baking powder until fully blended.

7 Mix in the walnuts.

8 Pour into the lined baking tin and bake for approx 25–30 minutes, the outside should be cracked and the inside should be sticky but firm.

9 Leave to cool and then slice into squares.

DIFFICULTY LEVEL	PREPARATION TIME	COOKING TIME	SERVES
MODERATE	20 MINUTES	25–30 MINUTES	6

Lieutenant Mike McClellan
Former Army Officer

My Hero

Private Frederick Hitch VC

Private Hitch won his VC for 'courageous conduct … holding … at all costs a most dangerous post, raked in reverse by the enemy's fire' at the Battle of Rorke's Drift in 1879, aged 22. He was shot in the shoulder, shattering his scapula, but continued fighting, his useless arm strapped to his side. Then in a further extraordinary action he carried patients to safety from the hospital (on fire and in danger of being overrun) across a courtyard swept by enemy fire – with thirty-seven pieces of smashed bone in his shoulder. Patched up with rudimentary surgery, he continued to serve fellow soldiers with ammunition until eventually passing out from loss of blood.

After military service, Hitch became a London taxi cab driver, an unassuming role for a man of such gallantry. He died aged fifty-six, poor and living alone, but his funeral was far from anonymous, accompanied as it was by a procession of taxis bringing the London streets to a standstill on its way to his burial place in Chiswick.

His story sticks with me for so many reasons: his bravery in staying at his post when most people would consider it suicide; his continued fighting despite horrific wounds and unimaginable pain; his return to almost obscurity; but perhaps chiefly his selfless efforts to help his invalid comrades to safety at great personal danger.

He was the type of person who, when every nerve screams 'save yourself', calmly takes stock and coolly looks after others before himself. British military history is full of brave and heroism, but it is the very human action of caring for others, amidst all that horror and violence, that sets Frederick Hitch VC apart.

When recounting his tale, Hitch said, 'Anyone else would have done the same in my position.' I'm sure we would like to think that, should we face great challenges, we would 'not be found wanting'. It is the fear that we might that drives us to better ourselves.

Yummy Mummy's Truffles

Ingredients

500g mixed dried fruit
4–6 tbsp dark rum
125g plain dark chocolate
125g plain cooking chocolate
100g butter
150g digestive biscuits
50g icing sugar
desiccated coconut or
cocoa powder (optional)

Method

1 Soak the fruit in the rum for 2–3 hours (or overnight).

2 Melt the chocolate and butter together, until all the chocolate has just melted. (This can be done over a pan of very hot water with a bowl sat on, with the chocolate and butter in.)

3 While the chocolate is melting, crush the biscuits into crumbs and add to the melted chocolate and butter.

4 Now, add the fruit and icing sugar until evenly mixed.

5 Chill the mixture for 15 minutes.

6 Roll into balls and you can either roll in coconut, coco powder or leave plain for a variety of truffles.

7 Place into truffle papers and leave to set in the fridge for 30 minutes.

DIFFICULTY LEVEL	PREPARATION TIME	COOKING TIME	SERVES
EASY	20 MINUTES	0	8–10

Stephen Fry
Actor, Comedian, Writer, TV Presenter

My Hero
Guy Gibson

Guy Penrose Gibson VC, DSO & Bar, DFC & Bar was the first Commanding Officer of the RAF's 617 Squadron, which he led in the 'Dambusters' raid, in 1943, resulting in the destruction of two large dams in the Ruhr area. The mission was as contentious as it was daring, but there is no doubt Gibson showed exceptional leadership, distinctive character and incomparable nerve to succeed. I am fortunate to be involved in the writing of a screenplay for Peter Jackson's new version of the Dambusters.

Honey Buns

Ingredients

2 eggs
75g caster sugar
1 tsp soft brown sugar
pinch of salt
100g self-raising flour
1 tsp baking powder
90g cooled, melted butter
1 tbsp honey, plus extra, for glazing

Method

1 Whisk the eggs and sugar together, using an electric whisk, until the mix has doubled in size.

2 Sift the flour, baking powder and salt and fold thoroughly into the eggs. Mix very gently and slowly, not to lose the air you have in the eggs.

3 Leave the mix to rest for 30 minutes, and then gently stir in the honey and butter.

4 Bake in greased tins (muffin tins are good) at 180C / 350F / Gas Mark 4 for 18–20 minutes.

5 When cooked, put on a cooling wire, melt the extra honey and glaze the buns with it, once they are cooled.

Enjoy with a nice cup of tea.

DIFFICULTY LEVEL	PREPARATION TIME	COOKING TIME	SERVES
EASY	10 MINS + 30 MINS RESTING TIME	20 MINUTES	10–12 SMALL CAKES

Private Harry Patch
The Last Surviving Tommy

My Hero
The Unknown German Soldier

I'm 110 years old. That's not bad going, is it?

I've seen a lot in my life, most of it good. But too many people come to me just because of a few months I spent in the trenches when I was a teenager. They ask me all sorts of questions. I've been asked the most detailed questions about life in the trenches. So I was a little bit doubtful when one of my friends came to me and said, "Ere 'Arry, there's this crazy bloke from the Royal Flying Corps wants your favourite nosh for your hero." 'Well,' I said. 'Seems a bloody stupid thing to ask me. Damned if I know a whelk from a Whiz Bang. But I'll give it some thought.' So I gave it some thought and this is my favourite recipe, and my reasons for choosing it. And my hero? Perhaps I'd have cooked him our Regimental pie. When we were in the trenches, it was easy to get some ingredients, but not some others. Take Bully Beef. We had loads of that. We had so much we used to lob it at the bosche. The buggers used to lob it straight back to us. Pastry, eggs, fresh milk, some good quality flour – that was a different matter altogether. They were available only from the Officers' dugout immediately after hamper delivery from Harrods.

As I said, I'm 110 and going strong. I have plenty of memories. Most are good, but some are not. I remember my school chums who went to war and didn't return. I remember the three members of my Lewis Gun Team …. I remember that brave German soldier.

They were my real heroes. For ninety years I've paid respect to them 'At the going down of the sun, and in the morning'.

Duke of Cornwall's Light Infantry Pie
Ingredients

Pastry:
600g plain flour
300g margarine (chilled)
50g caster sugar
3 eggs
1 tsp vanilla essence

Filling:
6 cooking apples
50g butter
6 kiwi fruit
100g caster sugar
egg to brush the top

Duke of Cornwall's Light Infantry Pie

(otherwise known as Patch Pie – created by the Food For Heroes chefs in honour of Private Harry Patch)

DIFFICULTY LEVEL	PREPARATION TIME	COOKING TIME	SERVES
MODERATE	40 MINUTES	40 MINUTES	6–8

This recipe is a slightly adapted version of the Duke of Cornwall's Light Infantry Pie – owing to the shortage of Bully Beef ninety years on since the end of WWI!

Method

1 First, to make the pastry, sift the flour into a large bowl and cut the margarine into cubes and rub into the flour, using your fingertips until the mix resembles breadcrumbs. Whisk up the eggs with the sugar and add to the mix with the vanilla. Mix in and bring the pastry together to a dough. If the mix is too dry, add a little milk to bring it together. Knead the pastry for a couple of minutes and then chill for 30 minutes.

2 While the pastry is chilling, you can make the filling (!). First peel the apples and cut into 1-inch wedges. Melt the butter in a pan and add the apples, cooking for a few minutes. Peel and cut the kiwis into the same size; then add them to the mix and pour in the sugar. Stir carefully, so as not to break up the fruit and set aside off the heat.

3 Take the pastry out of the fridge and knead for a few minutes to make it pliable.

4 Divide into two parts: put a quarter of the pastry to one side and roll out the rest to around 1cm thickness. Use this to line a 10-inch flan case, leaving any excess overhanging. Now put the fruit filling into the case. Roll out the remaining pastry and moisten the lip of the pastry case with some of the eggs. Put the lid on the pie, pushing the pastry down to join the top and bottom and cut off the excess. Use the excess to make a decoration for the top; you can even try the Duke of Cornwall Light Infantry cap badge! Brush the top of the pie with the beaten egg.

5 Cook the pie in a preheated oven at 180C / 350F / Gas Mark 4 for 30–40 minutes.

You can eat this hot, warm or cold; enjoy it with ice cream, cream or anything you like.

PRIVATE HARRY PATCH

Henry John Patch was born near Bath in 1898 during the reign of Queen Victoria. He enjoyed a typical country childhood in a caring family, getting into scrapes with his many childhood friends. Somehow or other he managed to acquire enough education to be able to start learning the plumbing trade.

The First World War started when Harry was 16. He didn't want to join the forces as a brother had told him what it was like and urged him to stay at home as long as he could. It was only the introduction of conscription which led to Harry joining the Army and being shipped to France and Belgium in the summer of 1917.

Between June and September 1917, Harry served at Ypres as a Lewis gunner in the 7th Duke of Cornwall's Light Infantry. He saw a great deal of action in the Third Battle of Ypres, (often called the Battle of Passchendaele) particularly around Langemarck and Pilkem Ridge. Harry did not want to kill the enemy and in the heat of battle chose to disable rather than kill a German soldier attacking his Lewis team.

At the end of September 1917, a German shell burst among Harry's Lewis gun team as they returned from action. Three of the five man team were killed; Harry was injured and one member of the team was unscathed. Harry was taken to a field hospital where a piece of shrapnel was removed from his left thigh without the benefit of anaesthetic.

After the war, Harry returned to his trade as a plumber and married the young girl he had met while convalescing after the Battle of Passchendaele. They were married in 1919 and had two sons. His wife died in 1976 and his sons have also predeceased him. Harry married again in 1980 and his second wife died in 1984.

Harry retired in 1963 and in 1996 moved to a residential home in Somerset, where he still lives.

Harry did not speak of his experiences during the First World War until 1998. For 80 years he had remained silent. Only the persuasiveness of Richard Van Emden, a military historian, enabled Harry's story to be told.

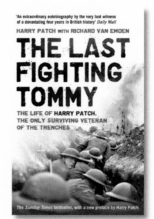

Harry's book The Last Fighting Tommy co-written with Richard Van Emden, gives a wonderful and comprehensive insight into Harry's life.

Harry Patch with Richard Van Emden,
The Last Fighting Tommy, Published by Bloomsbury

Acknowledgements

thank you to everyone

The Food for Heroes chefs headed by Sgt Dawn Bailey: Cpl Dave Johnston, Cpl Shane Rees, SAC Dave Butler; Sgt Fintan Jordan; Cpl Paul Adams; Cpl Danny Wilson and especially Cpl Fran Allen who stepped in to cover Dawn while she was in Afghanistan last summer. Thank you so much for your efforts, particularly over our mad three months at the end of 2008. You really are a hugely talented group of people.
Paul Gayler and Lucy Miller for their leadership and support in generating the chefs' contributions.

The Food for Heroes photographers headed by SAC Claire Mainwaring and Cpl Shaun Buxton: Sgt Michael Scraggs; Cpl Michael Jones; SAC Tim White; SAC Lynny Cash; SAC Chan Cooke. You should all be extremely proud of your contribution; the images look amazing and have really brought the book to life.

I hope you all are as proud of what we have produced as I am; it has been a pleasure to work with you all.

Our partners and families for your continuous support and for not showing how bored with cookery books and heroes you must really be by now.

All of our bosses who have been so patient, allowing us the time to put the book together.

Bryn and Emma Parry and all of the Help for Heroes team who are the real inspiration behind this book. The work that you have done over the past 18 months has been nothing short of extraordinary. Thank you for letting us be part of it.

Hazel, Bob, Alison, Luisa and all of the rest of the Accent Press team for your belief in our project. Jayne of Red Dot Design for the design and your patience.

Our printers, Butler, Tanner and Dennis, and their suppliers, for trimming all costs to the bone in order to maximize our charity contribution.

Group Captains David Stubbs and David Cass, Station Commanders of RAF Aldergrove for your continued support throughout the project.

Wg Cdr Mark Gilligan, Sqn Ldr Del McAllister, Fg Off Guy Wilton and Fg Off McGinley for supporting us when we needed help.

Jim Pullen for setting up and running our website.

All of the agents, personal secretaries, publicity managers et al who so kindly acted on behalf of their clients in contributing to the book.

Last but not least, all the contributors for giving up your precious time to provide the content of the book. And, yes, I know that I was lying when I said it would only take 10 minutes of your time ... sorry!

who made it possible

INDEX

Ackril, Kate 194

Admiral's Pie 57

Aisleyne 38

Alexander the Great 182

Ali, Muhammad 8, 98

Allen, Ranger Andy 114, 116

Allen, Corporal Francesca 194

Almonds
    Spicy Chicken with Almonds and Apricots Pitta Pocket 27

Anielewicz, Major Mordechai 4

Apollo 11 Crew 80

Apple
    Apple Crumble 191
    Banger and Scrumpy Pie 187
    Duke of Cornwall's Light Infantry Pie 233
    Fresh Fruit Salad with Chocolate Chip Ice Cream 215
    Hero Bear's Apple, Apricot and Honey Pie 201

Apple Crumble 191

Apricot
    Herby Couscous Salad 33
    Hero Bear's Apple, Apricot and Honey Pie 201
    Moroccan Lamb Tagine 137
    Spicy Chicken with Almonds and Apricots Pitta Pocket 27

Atha, Group Captain Stuart 208

Atkin, Stephanie 92

Atkin, Corporal Steve 92

Atkins, Dame Eileen 2

Attenborough, Sir David 226

Bacon
    Full Traditional English Fry-Up 19

Baked Figs with Walnuts and Blue Cheese 3

Baked Salmon with Lemon Hollandaise 63

Bader, Sir Douglas 184

Bailey, Sergeant Dawn 82

Banana
    Banoffi Pancakes 203
    Lovely Loaders' Loaf! (Banana and Walnut Loaf) 223

Band, Admiral Sir Jonathon 72

Banger and Scrumpy Pie 187

Banoffi Pancakes 203

Beans
    Crocked Tortillas with Chicken and Beans 99
    Full Traditional English Fry-Up 19
    Jamaican Red Pea Soup with Dumplings 39
    The Nimrod MR2 Honkers Stew 175
    Spitfire Cassoulet 185

Beef 143
    See also:
    Greek-style Burgers 29
    The Hungry Man's Chilli Tortillas 23

Beef Wellington 161

Beharry, Lance-Corporal Johnson 118

Bennett, Andrew 212

Berners-Lee, Sir Tim 132

Berries
    Fresh Fruit Salad with Chocolate Chip Ice Cream 215
    Gooseberry Crumble 199
    Raspberry Pavlova and Cream 221
    Strawberry Conde 219

Berry, Fred 224

Berry, Lieutenant Jim 224

Black Lamb 135

Blackadder, Edmund 134

Blair, Squadron Leader John 104, 106

Blair, Tony 46

Bland, Jeff 64

Blanks, Colonel Ian 180

Blue cheese
    Baked Figs with Walnuts and Blue Cheese 3

Boodle's Orange Fool 211

Boston Non-Clam Chowder 53

Botham, Sir Ian 160

Bowman, Flight Sergeant Alan 30

Braised Pheasant with Root Vegetables and Redcurrant Jelly 183

Brie Stuffed Chicken with Sweet Potato Mash 81

The British Armed Forces 214

Britton, Fern 198

INDEX

Broadbent, Jim 112
Brown, Gordon 172
Brunel, Isambard Kingdom 122
Burns, Right Reverend Thomas Matthew 56

Caesar, Julius 150
Cake
    Banoffi Pancakes 203
    Boodle's Orange Fool 211
    Raspberry Pavlova and Cream 221
    Sticky Toffee Stout Pudding 197
    Vanilla Chocolate Brownies 227
Cambodia mine victim 218
Cameron, David 118
Campbell, Donald 154
Charles, John 210
Charlton, Sir Bobby 212
Cheese
    Admiral's Pie 57
    Baked Figs with Walnuts and Blue Cheese 3
    Banger and Scrumpy Pie 187
    Brie Stuffed Chicken with Sweet Potato Mash 81
    Fish Lovers' Lasagne 73
    Goats Cheese and Red Onion Tart 49
    Greek-style Burgers 29
    Home-made Meatballs with an Italian Sauce and Pasta 169
    Jack's Spaghetti Bolognese 165
    Lasagne 147
    Mucked-Up Cheese 15
    'Nutter' not a Chicken 31
    Pan-fried Halloumi 35
    Prawns with Tomato and Feta 75
  Chequers Steak Pie 173
Chicken
    Brie Stuffed Chicken with Sweet Potato Mash 81
    Chicken Noodle Soup 5
    Chicken Satay with Pemmican 101
    Chicken Smiley 83
    Chicken Supreme 95
    Chicken Tikka with Savoury Rice 93

    Chinese Chicken Curry with Egg Fried Rice and Prawn Crackers 105
    Crocked Tortillas with Chicken and Beans 99
    Dad's Chicken Korma 85
    Herby Couscous Salad 33
    Honey and Mustard Chicken 91
    Murgh Pilow served with Dahee Chaat 89
    'Nutter' not a Chicken 31
    Spicy Chicken with Almonds and Apricots Pitta Pocket 27
    Turkey or Chicken Boobs 87
    Viscount Slim's Cold Chicken in a Curried Mayonnaise 103
    The World's Hottest Chicken Curry 97
Chicken Noodle Soup 5
Chicken Satay with Pemmican 101
Chicken Smiley 83
Chicken Supreme 95
Chicken Tikka with Savoury Rice 93
Chickpeas
    Murgh Pilow served with Dahee Chaat 89
    North African Lamb with Ginger and Chickpeas 121
Chilli
    Chicken Noodle Soup 5
    Chicken Satay with Pemmican 101
    Chicken Tikka with Savoury Rice 93
    Dad's Chicken Korma 85
    Fish Jalfrezi 61
    Fresh Tagliatelle with Leek and Prawns 69
    The Hungry Man's Chilli Tortillas 23
    Kedgeree 67
    Lamb Samosa and Onion Bhaji Served with a Mint Dressing 139
    Moroccan Lamb Tagine 137
    Murgh Pilow served with Dahee Chaat 89
    North African Lamb with Ginger and Chickpeas 121
    Salmon, Potato and Pasta Broth 55
    Slow Roast Shoulder of Lamb 119
    Spicy Lentil Curry 41
    Sweet and Sour Pork 113
    Tex Mex Spicy Balls with Tomato Salsa 155
    Vietnamese Rice Paper Rolls 65

The World's Hottest Chicken Curry 97

Chinese Chicken Curry with Egg Fried Rice and Prawn Crackers 105

Chips

    Egg and Chip Banjo 17

Chocolate

    Fresh Fruit Salad with Chocolate Chip Ice Cream 215

    Vanilla Chocolate Brownies 227

    Yummy Mummy's Truffles 229

Churchill, Sir Winston 144

Cinnamon

    Spiced Plum and Walnut Crumble with Cinnamon Ice Cream 193

Clarke, Air Commodore Charles 220

Clegg, Nick 122

Coastal Comfort Soup 11

Cobham, Sir Alan 104

Coconut

    Dad's Chicken Korma 85

    Jamaican Red Pea Soup with Dumplings 39

    Thai King Prawn Curry with Thai Fragrant Rice 71

    Thai Sticky Rice and Mango 207

Cod

    Admiral's Pie 57

    Fish Lovers' Lasagne 73

    Panga Tandoori 77

Coe, Lord Sebastian 74

Conlan, Warrant Officer 2 Kieron 60

Connolly, Billy 158

Courgette

    Fillet of Beef on a Toasted Brioche 153

Couscous

    Herby Couscous Salad 33

Crab

    Vietnamese Rice Paper Rolls 65

Cream

    Fresh Fruit Salad with Chocolate Chip Ice Cream 215

    Raspberry Pavlova and Cream 221

    Spiced Plum and Walnut Crumble with Cinnamon Ice Cream 193

Crocked Tortillas with Chicken and Beans 99

Crumble

    Apple Crumble 191

    Gooseberry Crumble 199

    Spiced Plum and Walnut Crumble with Cinnamon Ice Cream 193

Cucumber

    Herby Couscous Salad 33

Cunningham, Admiral Sir Andrew Browne 72

Curry

    Chicken Tikka with Savoury Rice 93

    Chinese Chicken Curry with Egg Fried Rice and Prawn Crackers 105

    Dad's Chicken Korma 85

    Lamb Biriani 131

    Thai King Prawn Curry with Thai Fragrant Rice 71

    Viscount Slim's Cold Chicken in a Curried Mayonnaise 103

    The World's Hottest Chicken Curry 97

Custard

    Gibson's Just Dessert 209

    Steamed Syrup Sponge and Homemade Custard 195

Dad's Chicken Korma 85

Dannatt, General Sir Richard 102

David, Elizabeth 58

Dench, Dame Judi 48

Dover, Senior Aircraftman Adam 152

Dover, Murielle 152

Duck

    Spitfire Cassoulet 185

Duke, Flight Lieutenant Paul 52

Duke of Cornwall's Light Infantry Pie 233

Dumpling

    Jamaican Red Pea Soup with Dumplings 39

Dunse, Corporal Richie 54

Duran, Roberto 18

Durnford, Captain Sally 120

Egg

    Chinese Chicken Curry with Egg Fried Rice and Prawn

INDEX

Crackers 105

Egg and Chip Banjo 17

Egg Mayonnaise Sandwiches and Homemade Crisps 21

Full Traditional English Fry-Up 19

Egg and Chip Banjo 17

Egg Mayonnaise Sandwiches and Homemade Crisps 21

Feta cheese

Greek-style Burgers 29

Prawns with Tomato and Feta 75

Fiennes, Sir Ranulph 168, 180

Figs

Baked Figs with Walnuts and Blue Cheese 3

Fillet of Beef on a Toasted Brioche 153

Fish

Admiral's Pie 57

Baked Salmon with Lemon Hollandaise 63

Boston Non-Clam Chowder 53

Coastal Comfort Soup 11

Fish Jalfrezi 61

Hot and Sour Soup with Fish 9

Kedgeree 67

Panga Tandoori 77

Salmon, Potato and Pasta Broth 55

Sea bass with a Delicate Lemon Risotto 59

Fish Jalfrezi 61

Fish Lovers' Lasagne 73

Forsyth, Bruce 144

Forsyth's Steak Dijon 145

Fox, Edward 76

Fox, Ranger Grant 114

Fresh Fruit Salad with Chocolate Chip Ice Cream 215

Fresh Tagliatelle with Leek and Prawns 69

Fry, Stephen 230

Full Traditional English Fry-Up 19

Game and Sausages 177

Gandhi, Mahatma 2, 46

Gayler, Corporal Lee Daniel 84

Gayler, Paul 84

George, Gillian 186, 188

Gibson, Guy 208, 230

Gibson's Just Dessert 209

Gillan, Lance Corporal Nick 202, 204–5

Gilligan, Wing Commander Mark 158

Ginger

North African Lamb with Ginger and Chickpeas 121

Gladwin, Peter 58

Goats Cheese

Goats Cheese and Red Onion Tart 49

Goats Cheese and Red Onion Tart 49

Goodman, Flight Lieutenant Michelle 66, 146, 148–9

Gooseberry Crumble 199

Gorman, Flight Lieutenant John 190

Greek-style Burgers 29

Grey-Thompson, Dame Tanni 160

Grohl, Dave 60

Grosvenor, Major-General Gerald Cavendish 182

Haddock

Admiral's Pie 57

Coastal Comfort Soup 11

Panga Tandoori 77

Hadley, Tony 196

Haggan, Lance Corporal Chris 94

Halloumi

Pan-fried Halloumi 35

Ham

Baked Figs with Walnuts and Blue Cheese 3

Pease Pudding 111

Hamilton, Lieutenant Agnes 138, 140–1

Harriott, Ainsley 32

Hatton, Ricky 18

Hazelnut

Vanilla-Creamed Tapioca 213

Herb-crumbed Pork with Pasta and Tomato Sauce 109

Herby Couscous Salad 33

Herdwick Mutton with Creamy Onion Sauce and Buttery Mash 129

Hero Bear 200

Hero Bear's Apple, Apricot and Honey Pie 201

Hero Pie 157

Hitch, Private Frederick 228

Holmes, Dame Kelly 74

Home-made Meatballs with an Italian Sauce and Pasta 169

Honey

    Hero Bear's Apple, Apricot and Honey Pie 201

    Honey and Mustard Chicken 91

    Honey Buns 231

Honey and Mustard Chicken 91

Honey Buns 231

Hot and Sour Soup with Fish 9

Howard, Kirsty 82

Humphreys, Flight Lieutenant Tom 132

The Hungry Man's Chilli Tortillas 23

Hutton, John 124

Ice cream

    Fresh Fruit Salad with Chocolate Chip Ice Cream 215

    Spiced Plum and Walnut Crumble with Cinnamon Ice Cream 193

Jack's Spaghetti Bolognese 165

Jackson, Colin 216

Jamaican Red Pea Soup with Dumplings 39

James, Jimmy 220

Jason, Sir David 80

Judd, Royal Australian Signals Corporal Colin 'Doc' 108

'KC' 136

Keable, Sub-Lieutenant Donald 162

Kedgeree 67

Kemp, Ross 202, 214

Kendall, Wing Commander Seb 206

Kenny, Lance Corporal Andrew 114

Kidney

    Steak and Kidney Pudding 167

King, Dr Martin Luther, Jr. 110

King prawn

    Thai King Prawn Curry with Thai Fragrant Rice 71

Kiwi

    Duke of Cornwall's Light Infantry Pie 233

Lacey, Private Frederick 166

Ladyman, Stephen 154

Lamb 117

Lamb Biriani 131

Lamb Samosa and Onion Bhaji Served with a Mint Dressing 139

Lancaster, Leading Aircraftsman Raymond 14

Langoustine

    Coastal Comfort Soup 11

Lasagne 147

Le Fanu, Admiral of the Fleet Sir Michael 162

Lee, Bruce 94

Leek

    Fresh Tagliatelle with Leek and Prawns 69

Lemon

    Baked Salmon with Lemon Hollandaise 63

    Lemon Tart 217

    Sea bass with a Delicate Lemon Risotto 59

Lemon Tart 217

Lentil

    Spicy Lentil Curry 41

Liddell, Eric 172

Lime

    Vietnamese Rice Paper Rolls 65

Little, Major Jake 168

Little Venice 38

Loader, Lady Alison 222

Lomu, Jonah 88

Lovely Loaders' Loaf! (Banana and Walnut Loaf) 223

Lynn, Dame Vera 86

Mandela, Nelson 48

Mango

    Thai Sticky Rice and Mango 207

Mayne, Blair 'Paddy' 136

INDEX

Mayson, Tom Fletcher 124

McClellan, Lieutenant Mike 228

McGregor, Ewan 170

McIndoe, Dr Sir Archibald 44

McNab, Andy 96

Mince and Tatties 159

Mint Lamb Chops with Roasted Shallots and Spinach Mash 123

Moon, Chris 218

Moroccan Lamb Tagine 137

Moroney, Private William 10

Mosimann, Anton 8

Mountbatten, Louis, 1st Earl Mountbatten of Burma 14, 138

Mucked-Up Cheese 15

Mum's Bakestones 225

Mum's Beef and Guinness Casserole 171

Murgh Pilow served with Dahee Chaat 89

Murray, Lieutenant Commander Andrew 'Tank' 22, 24–5

Murray, Sgt George Henry 22

Mushroom

    Hero Pie 157

    Roasted Vegetable Tarte Tatin 45

    Stuffed Flat Field Mushrooms 47

Mustard

    Forsyth's Steak Dijon 145

    Honey and Mustard Chicken 91

Nelson, Admiral Lord 56

The Nimrod MR2 Honkers Stew 175

Noodles

    Chicken Noodle Soup 5

North African Lamb with Ginger and Chickpeas 121

Nuts

    Baked Figs with Walnuts and Blue Cheese 3

    Lovely Loaders' Loaf! (Banana and Walnut Loaf) 223

    'Nutter' not a Chicken 31

    Spiced Plum and Walnut Crumble with Cinnamon Ice Cream 193

    Spicy Chicken with Almonds and Apricots Pitta Pocket 27

'Nutter' not a Chicken 31

Obama, Barack 32

O'Donoghue, General Sir Kevin 70

Onion

    Goats Cheese and Red Onion Tart 49

    Herdwick Mutton with Creamy Onion Sauce and Buttery Mash 129

    Lamb Samosa and Onion Bhaji Served with a Mint Dressing 139

    Roasted Vegetable Tarte Tatin 45

Orange

    Boodle's Orange Fool 211

    Fresh Fruit Salad with Chocolate Chip Ice Cream 215

Pancakes

    Banoffi Pancakes 203

Pan-fried Halloumi 35

Panga Tandoori 77

Pankhurst, Emmeline 34

Parkinson, Lance Bombardier Ben 16

Parry, Bryn 16

Parry, Emma 156

Pasta

    Fish Lovers' Lasagne 73

    Fresh Tagliatelle with Leek and Prawns 69

    Herb-crumbed Pork with Pasta and Tomato Sauce 109

    Home-made Meatballs with an Italian Sauce and Pasta 169

    Jack's Spaghetti Bolognese 165

    Lasagne 147

    Prawns with Tomato and Feta 75

    Salmon, Potato and Pasta Broth 55

Patch, Private Harry 40, 232, 234

Patch Pie 233

Payton, Walter 26

Pear

    Fresh Fruit Salad with Chocolate Chip Ice Cream 215

Pease Pudding 111

Pheasant

    Braised Pheasant with Root Vegetables and Redcurrant Jelly 183

Pickwick Pie 151

Pie

Duke of Cornwall's Light Infantry Pie 233

Hero Bear's Apple, Apricot and Honey Pie 201

Lemon Tart 217

Pinner, Squadron Leader Al 184

Plum

Spiced Plum and Walnut Crumble with Cinnamon
Ice Cream 193

Pork 107

See also:

Banger and Scrumpy Pie 187

Full Traditional English Fry-Up 19

Rack of Lamb with Spinach 133

Spitfire Cassoulet 185

Pot Roast Venison 181

Potato

Admiral's Pie 57

Brie Stuffed Chicken with Sweet Potato Mash 81

Egg Mayonnaise Sandwiches and Homemade Crisps 21

Herdwick Mutton with Creamy Onion Sauce and
Buttery Mash 129

Mince and Tatties 159

Mint Lamb Chops with Roasted Shallots and
Spinach Mash 123

The Nimrod MR2 Honkers Stew 175

Pot Roast Venison 181

Salmon, Potato and Pasta Broth 55

Six-Hour Slow Braised Lamb Shoulder and
Champ Potato 127

Special Winter Lancashire Hot Pot 125

Poultry 79

See also:

Chicken Noodle Soup 5

Herby Couscous Salad 33

'Nutter' not a Chicken 31

Spicy Chicken with Almonds and Apricots Pitta Pocket 27

Prawn

Admiral's Pie 57

Boston Non-Clam Chowder 53

Chinese Chicken Curry with Egg Fried Rice and Prawn

Crackers 105

Fish Lovers' Lasagne 73

Fresh Tagliatelle with Leek and Prawns 69

Prawns with Tomato and Feta 75

Thai King Prawn Curry with Thai Fragrant Rice 71

Prawns with Tomato and Feta 75

Prince Charles 128

Prior, John 166

Prunes

Vanilla-Creamed Tapioca 213

Puddings and Baking 189

Pullen, Squadron Leader Jon 134

Quinlan, Jack 164

Quinlan, Flight Sergeant Paul 164

R2-D2 146

Rack of Lamb with Spinach 133

The RAF Nimrod Fleet 174, 176

Raspberry Pavlova and Cream 221

Ratia, Signalman Martin 108

Redgrave, Sir Steve 54, 62

The Rescue Services 174

Rice

Chicken Satay with Pemmican 101

Chicken Smiley 83

Chicken Supreme 95

Chicken Tikka with Savoury Rice 93

Chinese Chicken Curry with Egg Fried Rice and Prawn
Crackers 105

Honey and Mustard Chicken 91

Kedgeree 67

Murgh Pilow served with Dahee Chaat 89

Prawns with Tomato and Feta 75

Sea bass with a Delicate Lemon Risotto 59

Strawberry Conde 219

Thai King Prawn Curry with Thai Fragrant Rice 71

Thai Sticky Rice and Mango 207

Vietnamese Rice Paper Rolls 65

Rigg, Captain Dave 40, 42–3

Risotto
Sea bass with a Delicate Lemon Risotto 59
Roasted Vegetable Tarte Tatin 45

Roberts, Commander I T 110
Rusi Todiwala's Venison Sheek Kavaab 179

Salmon
Baked Salmon with Lemon Hollandaise 63
Coastal Comfort Soup 11
Salmon, Potato and Pasta Broth 55
Salmon, Potato and Pasta Broth 55

Sausage
Banger and Scrumpy Pie 187
Full Traditional English Fry-Up 19
Home-made Meatballs with an Italian Sauce and Pasta 169
The Nimrod MR2 Honkers Stew 175

Scallops
Boston Non-Clam Chowder 53
Fish Lovers' Lasagne 73

Schofield, Private Harry 90
Scott, Captain Robert Falcon 100
Sea bass with a Delicate Lemon Risotto 59

Seafood 51
See also:
Coastal Comfort Soup 11
Hot and Sour Soup with Fish 9

Shackleton, Ernest 96, 120
Shallots
Coastal Comfort Soup 11
Mint Lamb Chops with Roasted Shallots and Spinach Mash 123

Sheene, Barry 30
Sikorsky, Igor Ivor 130
Simson, Corporal Hannah 226
Sinatra, Frank 196
Six-Hour Slow Braised Lamb Shoulder and Champ Potato 127
Slater, Pete 68
Slim, Field Marshal The Viscount 70, 102, 206

Slow Roast Shoulder of Lamb 119
Snacks and Salads 13
Snellock, Squadron Leader Chris 66
Soup
See Starters and Soups
Special Winter Lancashire Hot Pot 125
Spiced Plum and Walnut Crumble with Cinnamon Ice Cream 193
Spicy Chicken with Almonds and Apricots Pitta Pocket 27
Spicy Lentil Curry 41
Spinach
Mint Lamb Chops with Roasted Shallots and Spinach Mash 123
Rack of Lamb with Spinach 133
Spitfire Cassoulet 185
Spitz, Mark 62
Sponge
Steamed Syrup Sponge and Homemade Custard 195
Starters and Soups 1
See also:
Jamaican Red Pea Soup with Dumplings 39
Steak
Chequers Steak Pie 173
Fillet of Beef on a Toasted Brioche 153
Forsyth's Steak Dijon 145
Hero Pie 157
Mum's Beef and Guinness Casserole 171
The Nimrod MR2 Honkers Stew 175
Steak and Kidney Pudding 167
Steak and Kidney Pudding 167
Steamed Syrup Sponge and Homemade Custard 195
Stew
The Nimrod MR2 Honkers Stew 175
Stewart, Jimmy 170
Sticky Toffee Stout Pudding 197
Stilton Cheese
'Nutter' not a Chicken 31
Stirrup, Sir Jock 150
Strawberry Conde 219
Street, Corporal Richard 98

Stroud-Turp, Lieutenant Colonel John 90

Stuffed Flat Field Mushrooms 47

Stuffed Pork Fillet with Pesto 115

Sullivan, Captain Eamonn 10

Sutton, Lieutenant Commander Rich 130

Sweet and Sour Pork 113

Sylvester, Warrant Officer Al 100

Szabo, Violette 156

Tanner, Chris 126

Tanner, James 126

Tapioca

    Vanilla-Creamed Tapioca 213

Tariq, Leading Hand Naheed 88

Tex Mex Spicy Balls with Tomato Salsa 155

Thai King Prawn Curry with Thai Fragrant Rice 71

Thai Sticky Rice and Mango 207

Thoburn, Steve 76

Thompson, Daley 216

Todiwala, Cyrus 178

Todiwala, Rustom Dhunjishaw 178

Toffee

    Banoffi Pancakes 203

    Sticky Toffee Stout Pudding 197

Tolstoy, Leo 112

Tomato

    Full Traditional English Fry-Up 19

    Herb-crumbed Pork with Pasta and Tomato Sauce 109

    Prawns with Tomato and Feta 75

    Tex Mex Spicy Balls with Tomato Salsa 155

Tombling, Chris 64

Torpy, Air Chief Marshal Sir Glen 192

Tortilla

    Crocked Tortillas with Chicken and Beans 99

    The Hungry Man's Chilli Tortillas 23

Trenchard, Lord Hugh, Marshal of the RAF 192

Truffles

    Yummy Mummy's Truffles 229

Tuna

    Fish Jalfrezi 61

Turkey

    Turkey or Chicken Boobs 87

Turkey or Chicken Boobs 87

Turner, Brian 210

The Ultimate Roast Beef and Yorkshire Pudding 163

Underhill, Captain Chris 28

The Unknown German Soldier 232

Vanilla Chocolate Brownies 227

Vanilla-Creamed Tapioca 213

Vegetarian 37

    See also:

        Egg and Chip Banjo 17

        Egg Mayonnaise Sandwiches and Homemade Crisps 21

        Lasagne 147

        Mucked-Up Cheese 15

        Pan-fried Halloumi 35

Venison

    Pot Roast Venison 181

    Rusi Todiwala's Venison Sheek Kavaab 179

    Spitfire Cassoulet 185

Vietnamese Rice Paper Rolls 65

Viscount Slim's Cold Chicken in a Curried Mayonnaise 103

Wallis, Sir Barnes 28

Walnuts

    Baked Figs with Walnuts and Blue Cheese 3

    Lovely Loaders' Loaf! (Banana and Walnut Loaf) 223

    Spiced Plum and Walnut Crumble with Cinnamon Ice Cream 193

Webb, Roy 52

Wenham-Jones, Jane 20

Weston, Simon 44

Whittle, Sir Frank 190

Widdecombe, The Rt. Hon. Ann 20

Wilcox, Paula 34

INDEX

Wilkinson, Jonny 26, 68

Winnie the Pooh 200

Wiseman, Warrant Officer Andrew 4, 6–7

The World's Hottest Chicken Curry 97

Worrall Thompson, Antony 128

Yoghurt

    Herby Couscous Salad 33

    Lamb Samosa and Onion Bhaji Served with a Mint Dressing 139

Yummy Mummy's Truffles 229